The Casino

Santa Catalina Island's
"Two Million Dollar Palace of Pleasure"

by Patricia Anne Moore

Published by

Preserving the rich cultural heritage of
Santa Catalina Island

Published by
Catalina Island Museum Society, Inc.
Philip K. Wrigley Publishing Fund
1 Casino Way, P.O. Box 366
Avalon, CA 90704

Explore and celebrate
Santa Catalina Island's history through
the Catalina Island Museum Store
310-510-2414

ISBN: 0-9720668-0-2

Contents

Dedication

This book is dedicated to Mr. and Mrs. Malcolm J. Renton, whose support and leadership sustained the Museum during the first thirty years of its existence.

A leading figure in Avalon's cultural life, Virginia Hill Renton was a founding member of the Catalina Island Museum Society in 1953 and played an active role in its direction for twenty-five years. Upon her retirement, she was elected President Emeritus and an Honorary Member of the Board of Trustees in Perpetuity. As a young Avalon school teacher in 1929, she danced in the Casino Ballroom and watched the first "talkie" films in Avalon Theatre.

In 1929, after graduation from Stanford University, Malcolm J. Renton became an assistant to his father, David M. Renton, who built the Casino for William Wrigley Jr. As executive vice president of the Santa Catalina Island Company from 1947 to 1975, he was intimately associated with the history of the building. A founding member of the Catalina Island Museum Society, he served actively on the Board of Trustees until 1982, Upon his retirement, he was elected an Honorary Member of the Board and continued thereafter to be a strong financial supporter of the Museum.

Malcolm J. Renton   Virginia Hill Renton

Acknowledgment

The original edition of this book, printed in 1979, was a Catalina Island Museum Society contribution to the 50th anniversary of the Casino. It became a reality because of the cooperation of many people. William Wrigley, grandson of the builder of the Casino, provided photographs and contributed a forward on behalf of his family, which has played such an important part in the history of Santa Catalina Island. Claude Brooks, then president of the Santa Catalina Island Company, made available photographs and information relating to the Casino. Interviews were conducted with Malcolm Renton, John Gabriel Beckman, Art LaShelle, Tommy Clements, Lank Menge, Wilfred F. Olsen, Kurt Houck, and members Harvey Heck, Gene Davis, Harold Donze, Paul Birk, and Bob Smith of the American Theatre Organ Society. Also generously sharing their knowledge were Joseph Arno, Jack Baptiste, Randall Duell, Donald R. Haney, Ford Harris, Arthur Meyerhoff Associates, Inc., M. B. Nichols, Ray Nichols, Maury Paul, Hal Rees, Lita Utal, and Johnny Windle. A major source of information was Dale Eisenhut, building superintendent from 1947 to 1980, who provided invaluable assistance. Researchers included Thelma Nowlin, Erika Kingett, Kathleen Johnson, and Charles M. Liddell, who conducted several interviews on the mainland that otherwise could not have been obtained. In 1979, I was the Museum's curator; in 1999, I had just retired as director/curator after 25 years with the Museum.

This second edition, printed in 2002, was produced with the assistance of a new generation of people graciously generous with their time and knowledge. Ronald C. Doutt, CEO of the Santa Catalina Island Company, provided information and access to the company's photo archives, and Audry Bierold facilitated my photo search there. Wayne Griffin, Executive Director of the Catalina Island Visitors Bureau and Chamber of Commerce, graciously provided Big Band information. Interviews were conducted with Robert D. Salisbury, Chee Ammen, Art Good, Glenn Finney, Malcolm Jones, Joe Caliva, Charles M. Liddell, Jim Spohn, and most important, Billy Delbert, Director of Casino Operations, who succeeded Dale Eisenhut as principal informant concerning happenings at the Casino during the 20 years between editions. My thanks go to Diane Conover, Bruce Moore, and especially Darlene Schmeckpepper for perusing 20 years of newspapers for information about the Casino. I am especially indebted to Stacey Otte, the new Director of the Museum, for her critical reading of the text and production coordination, and to Jeannine Pedersen, Curator of Collections, for scanning and organizing the photographs and generally shepherding the book through the publication process. Don Poyas for generously donating his professional talent and facilities and David Poyas for designing the cover. For this, the Museum Society is most grateful.

This little book represents the best information assembled at the time it went to press, but even as it was being printed, new facts and anecdotes were coming to light. Further information that will help improve its accuracy and comprehensiveness will be most welcome. Comments should be sent to the Curator, Catalina Island Museum, P. O. Box 366, Avalon, CA 90704.

Patricia Anne Moore
September 1999

Foreword to First Edition

The occasion of the Catalina Casino's 50th Anniversary in 1979 also marks the 60th anniversary of Wrigley family involvement in Santa Catalina Island. It was back in 1919 when my grandfather first purchased an interest in the Santa Catalina Island Company from the Banning family.

The construction and opening of the Catalina Casino in 1929 was a high point in a decade of development and growth spearheaded by William Wrigley Jr. Although my grandfather had the inspiration and enthusiasm to construct the magnificent Catalina Casino, my father, Philip K. Wrigley, was deeply involved in the concept of the structure. A few years prior to the architectural design of the Casino, he had seen a two-tiered building incorporating a theatre on the lower floor and ballroom dancing on the floor above in a single distinctive structure. He was impressed with this idea and suggested to his father that the architects consider a similar design for the proposed Catalina Casino.

The first decade of development of Catalina Island, with substantial family investment in the Santa Catalina Island Company, also marked the beginning of the Spanish motif and atmosphere that is still apparent in present-day Avalon. It was my father's great desire to see that Avalon and Catalina were always distinctive, unique and beautiful when compared to the stereotyped over-development of the mainland.

My father loved all that Catalina represented and was determined to preserve it as had his father before him. This not only applied to structures and landscaping but the overall preservation of Catalina's natural beauty for future generations. This dream was realized in 1975 by the forming of the Santa Catalina Island Conservancy. The Conservancy should protect the integrity and beauty of over 85 percent of the magnificent and unspoiled environment that nature has provided at Catalina.

Our family's deep involvement, both financial and personal, spans over 60 years. The Catalina Island Museum Society, of which both my father and mother were founding members, represents an important means to preserve the colorful history and heritage of Catalina Island.

William Wrigley

William Wrigley, the author of this foreword to the first edition of The Casino, actively promoted the preservation of Catalina Island's natural beauty and cultural heritage until his untimely death in 1999. During that time, he authorized a major renovation of Avalon's historic Casino Building so that it will provide a beautiful entertainment setting for the millions who will visit in the years to come. His son, William Wrigley Jr., the fourth generation of the family to be involved in Catalina Island, now continues this tradition of stewardship.

CIM Collection

William Wrigley Jr. 1861-1932

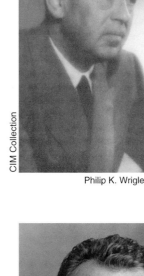

CIM Collection

Philip K. Wrigley 1894-1977

CIM Collection

William Wrigley 1933-1999

Courtesy of William Wrigley Jr. Company

William Wrigley Jr.
1963-

1 Introduction

The Santa Catalina Island Company, which figures prominently in this book as the owner of the Casino Building, was formed in 1894, by the brothers William, Joseph Brent, and Hancock Banning, who then owned the Island. William Wrigley Jr. purchased Catalina from the Bannings in 1919, sight unseen. Actually, he put up capital to help a friend, David Blankenhorn (a Pasadena real estate man), and his partners, who were interested in the island as a speculative venture. This syndicate then purchased majority stock in the Santa Catalina Island Company. However, Mr. Wrigley soon succumbed to Catalina's charms, and rather than see the Island subdivided and sold for quick profit, he bought out his new partners. For the last twelve years of his life, he devoted considerable thought and fortune to the development of Santa Catalina Island.

The interior of the Island that charmed Mr. Wrigley was much the same as seen today, although sheep rather than buffalo grazed on the hillsides. Avalon, however, must have been a much less impressive sight. Most of the large hotels had burned to the ground when a fire swept through the western half of the town in 1915. The Bannings had built Hotel St. Catherine in Descanso Canyon in 1918, and a large cafeteria, hotels, and other buildings were beginning to fill in the seared area of the town, but World War I slowed recovery. An era had passed, and people were already looking back to the good old days.

William Wrigley Jr. set to work to develop Catalina with the same energy and vision that characterized his rise in business. He visited the Island several times a year and was often seen riding around the town on his horse looking things over. He would also walk downtown regularly. Townspeople still fondly remember him dropping into their shops or offices with a cheery, "Well, what are you up to today?"

Catalina had been attracting tourists since the 1890's, when tent cities accommodated many of the families who enjoyed fishing, boating, hiking, golfing, bathing, and touring the interior by stagecoach or the undersea gardens by glass bottom boat. They also enjoyed dancing or listening to band concerts under the stars. Mr. Wrigley developed many of these at-

CIM Collection

William Wrigley Jr. 1919

tractions further, building a new dance pavilion and glass bottom boats, enlarging the golf course, and building a new visitors' country club. He also added attractions such as the Catalina Bird Park with its remarkable collection of exotic and colorful birds.

A far-sighted planner, Mr. Wrigley also attended to matters such as water supply by building Thompson Dam reservoir in Middle Canyon and improved cross channel transportation by purchasing the SS *Avalon* and building the SS *Catalina*—the Great White Steamers. (Captain William Banning, who continued his association with the island after the Wrigley purchase, brought the SS *Avalon* around from the East Coast through the Panama Canal.) The SS *Cabrillo*, acquired from the Bannings, completed the steamer fleet.

Advertising had played an important part in his career, and Mr. Wrigley applied his expertise to Catalina. When the Chicago Cubs were on the island for spring training, Catalina was in the minds of a great many sports fans. In 1927, a cross channel swim—the Wrigley Ocean Marathon—held the nation spellbound while the swimmers fought the cold channel currents. Millions of colorful postcards, with the Wrigley banner on the reverse, carried a message the world over— "In All the World No Trip Like This!".

For the thousands from the Midwest who flocked to the land of sunshine, the steamers provided their first ocean voyage, and Catalina remained a family resort, a place that the average person could afford. Mr. Wrigley hoped that the Island, with its equitable weather, would become a year round vacation spot. He attempted to stabilize the local population by providing year round employment. To this end, he developed Black Jack and Renton Mines (producing galena, a mixture of zinc, lead, and silver ore), expanded the rock quarries, and started industries such as a tile plant and furniture factory. He also embarked on an extensive building program. The first California Spanish style buildings on the Island date from this period.

The 1920's were good years for Catalina. The town was bustling with activity. As transportation, accommodations, and advertising improved, more people discovered the Island. The local newspaper, *The Catalina Islander*, which had been operated by Judge Ernest Windle since 1914, reported the increasing tourist counts—from 622,000 persons in 1926 to 700,000 in 1930. These were presumably steamer passenger counts and did not include airline passengers and yachting visitors.

The Island outgrew its old dance pavilions and theaters. As a climax to his ten-year development program, William Wrigley Jr. planned a magnificent theater and ballroom that would embody the new image of Catalina. The first dance pavilion he had built was called Sugarloaf Casino, using the term "casino" in its general sense as a "place of entertainment." The new structure was referred to as the New Casino, the symbol of the Island's future.

Since 1929, this building has been recognized around the world as the landmark of Catalina. It remains substantially the same both in appearance and in purpose as when it was built, and millions of people have been entertained within its walls. In 1990, the Santa Catalina Island Company began a major $1,535,000 restoration of the building, carefully maintaining as many of the original features as possible. Though it celebrated its 70th anniversary in 1999, the Catalina Casino stands ready to offer pleasure to millions more visitors in its historic ballroom and theater in the new millennium.

2 History of Casino Point

One sunny day early in 1928, William Wrigley Jr., accompanied by D. M. Renton, J. H. Patrick, and other company officials, including Transportation Department head, Johnny Windle, toured Avalon in his Pierce Arrow Touring Car, inspecting possible sites for the new Casino he planned to build. Johnny Windle recalled that when they reached the point, Mr. Wrigley stood for a moment surveying the area, then turned to D. M. Renton and said, "D. M., this is it." He then proceeded to describe the type of building he had in mind.

Sugarloaf Point, as it was then called, had always been the landmark of Avalon Bay. Sailors could identify their location by the distinctive sawtoothed ridge and the huge rock that jutted out of the water just beyond. Sugarloaf Rock, shaped like famous Sugarloaf Mountain in the bay at Rio de Janeiro, Brazil, captured the imagination of vacationers and appeared on a multitude of tinted, turn-of-the-century postcards mailed far and wide.

Avalon Bay at the Turn of the Century

Fireworks were set off from its height on July Fourth and other festive occasions. The more adventurous scaled its rough sides. In 1896, a stairway of 80 steps offered access to the timid. Tradition affirms that enterprising lads would loiter at the base of the stairway to help visitors who panicked when they attempted to descend—for a fee of 25¢.

Kelp beds flourished in the incredibly clear water around the point, attracting an exciting variety of marine life. In the 1890's, a trip in a glassbottom boat to view the fabled "undersea gardens" was a must. Attractions such as this were already drawing visitors to Santa Catalina from all over the world.

CIM Collection

Sugarloaf Rock

A tunnel blasted in the 1890's to neighboring Descanso Bay collapsed in 1906, altering the outline of the ridge. Now two peaks of rock were clearly visible—Big Sugarloaf and Little Sugarloaf. Hancock Banning had built a fine home in Descanso Bay, then called Banning Cove. The draw created by the collapsed tunnel was soon leveled and widened into a road, improving access to his home.

Sugarloaf Point was seriously considered by the Bannings as the site of a new hotel to replace the famed Hotel Metropole, destroyed in the 1915 fire. Big Sugarloaf was blasted away in 1917 in preparation for the new construction, but plans were changed and Hotel St. Catherine was built in Descanso Canyon. Blasting in those days was done with "black powder," which required both skill and courage.

William Wrigley Jr. chose the abandoned site on the point for Sugarloaf Casino. This octagonal, steel framed, stud and stucco structure, with two wings for concessions, was completed in 1920 and could accommodate about 250 dancing couples. The building served a variety of functions during its brief life. Malcolm Renton attended senior high school in its south wing (which previously boasted a Chinese Tea Room) until the new school buildings in Falls Canyon were completed. Caught up in the latest fad, he joined others for roller skating on the dance floor during 1926, an activity that resulted in broken bones among young and old.

Sugarloaf Casino under construction
(Chicago Cubs welcoming parade in foreground), 1920

An extensive planked deck surrounded the building and was furnished with benches – a favorite resting place between dances or while strolling between Avalon and Hotel St. Catherine. A freight wharf constructed on the Avalon side of the point in 1921 subsequently handled the bulk of construction materials barged from the mainland to supply the extensive building program D.M. Renton carried out for Mr. Wrigley.

This area remained the receiving point for the Island's heavy freight, including lumber, butane, and (in the early days) gasoline in 50-gallon

drums for the Standard Oil Station also located there, until the operation was removed to Pebbly Beach in 1958. Seaplanes–Curtiss F Flying Boats and bi-motored Sikorskys–also discharged their passengers at a float and ramp nearby until Hamilton Beach Am-

Sugarloaf Casino, late 1920's

phibian Airport opened in 1931.

Little Sugarloaf—
its weathered sides be-
coming more hazard-
ous for climbers, its
stairway declared un-
safe, then removed—
survived after
Sugarloaf Casino was
dismantled in February
of 1928. (The octago-
nal steel frame of the

Sugarloaf rock and deck of Sugarloaf Casino, 1927

dance pavilion was reassembled at Catalina Bird Park to make "the world's largest bird cage.")

However, during the ensuing year, the walls of the new Casino rose higher and higher and soon dwarfed the venerable rock. The whole perspective of the point changed. In March of 1929, the old rock was blasted away to improve the view of the magnificent new building. Sugarloaf Rock would have been located about where the flagpole is now. This 92 ft., 8 in. steel pole replaced the original flagpole in 1946.

The New Casino, 1929

CIM Collection

The United States Maritime Service trained in Avalon during World War II (Opening Ceremony for USMS Training School on Casino Point, December 1942)

Sugarloaf Point was built up to become a parking lot. Phoenix date palm trees were part of the original landscaping. The tall Washingtonian palms were added in 1934 by Philip K. Wrigley as part of a beautification project. The Washingtonian palms at the theater entrance were planted in 1948.

World War II temporarily altered the historic view. A battery of anti-aircraft guns was mounted on the point and a large wooden building constructed in the parking area as an armory. The bow of a ship was constructed on the wharf to help merchant seaman trainees practice loading cargo and maneuvers such as "abandon ship." These wartime additions were removed in 1946. Only the cement bases for the gun emplacements remain as evidence.

CIM Collection

The Diving Bell, 1951-1961

The undersea gardens off Casino Point continued to delight visitors. In 1951, the daring were able to view them from beneath the surface when a diving bell was constructed on the point. Viewers slowly descended among the fish and kelp in a giant sphere, then popped to the surface with a thrill at the end of the "dive." The diving bell, operated by Jack and Phyllis Wyvell, was removed in 1961, but snorkelers and scuba divers continue to descend beneath the surface to enjoy the rich panorama of undersea life in the area, now an underwater park.

Casino Point took on its present aspect in 1964, when the sea wall was reinforced and a short breakwater or "mole" was built, using rock from Pebbly Beach quarry, to provide protection to Avalon Bay during winter northeast storms. At its tip is a navigation symbol maintained by the U.S. Coast Guard to aid yachtsmen.

Children now enjoy climbing among the boulders or investigating a huge 18th century anchor salvaged from the bay and placed on the point in 1952. It is flanked by soapstone boulders bearing scars made by Catalina's Indians during their manufacture of soapstone bowls at a quarry near Empire Landing down the coast. These boulders were also placed on the point in 1952.

CIM Collection

The Casino at night

3   The Casino Architecture

At Sugarloaf Point, William Wrigley Jr. envisioned a large building of Moorish style with a ballroom over a theater, a concept suggested by his son, Philip K. Wrigley. It remained for the architects Walter Webber and Sumner A. Spaulding to design a suitable structure. Randall Duell, who now heads a firm that designs major recreation parks, worked on the Casino as a young assistant to Rowland Crawford, head architectural designer for Webber and Spaulding. He recalls that the restrictions given by Mr. Wrigley were two: neither Sugarloaf Rock on the point nor Mrs. Wrigley's flower garden near the base of the cliff were to be disturbed. This, in effect, determined the size of the building.

Perhaps the process by which Mr. Wrigley's idea was translated into a design is best described in the words of architect Webber: "This point of land being triangular in shape dictated a circular building as the most logical. The diameter of the building is the maximum which would fit upon this site, and the dance hall, directly over the theater on the ground floor, required a greater area than the theater, developing to a large extent the external character of the structure.

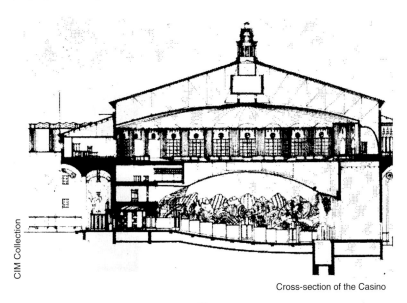

CIM Collection

Cross-section of the Casino

17

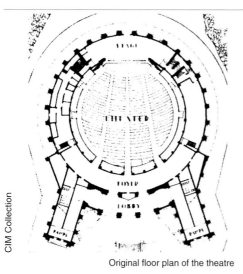

Original floor plan of the theatre

"The theater is almost a true hemisphere springing from the floor, with penetrations at front and back for proscenium and projection, within a cylinder of approximately 50 ft. greater diameter. The space surrounding this inverted bowl is in three stories, enlarging toward the center as they approach the apex of the dome, the dance hall above covering the whole cylinder section.

The desire for a dance hall as large as possible inspired the idea of a complete overhanging balcony [14 ft.] wide around the building at this floor level for circulation. Thus, the general plan was dictated by location and the utilitarian requirements for which the structure was purposed.

The theater auditorium being [138 ft.] wide required a ceiling height of approximately [43 ft.]. This raised the floor level of the ballroom 45 ft. above the entrance level of the street. The problem of asking people to climb four or five stories was a trying one. Elevators did not seem practical for such large crowds. Then Mr. Wrigley himself suggested ramps as used in his ball parks. These ramps when decided upon fit perfectly in the two corners of the triangular site left after the circular building was located."[1]

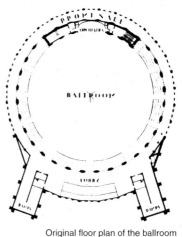

Original floor plan of the ballroom

The entire structure is designed on a cantilever plan. Two 178 ft. girders, weighing 50 tons each, span the building at right angles. It is trussed vertically and braced horizontally with three flat trusses. Six semi-cantilever trusses radiating from the center give the theater a domed ceiling and support the floor of the ballroom above. Columns and beams of steel, fireproofed with concrete, support the main weight of the roof and all floor weight except that of the ballroom. The exterior buttresses carry a vertical load.

The steel frame is encased in concrete poured in place, not precast, rendering the building on its 40 ft. sunken foundations an impressive monolith. In 1962, as the Avalon building most likely to survive disaster, it was designated a Civil Defense Shelter. The emphasis has since changed from war to natural catastrophe, but emergency supplies for two weeks are still stored in its many cubbyholes. If needed, the building will serve as an alternative base of government for the City of Avalon and will be available to the Red Cross for relief efforts.

What might be termed a social disaster occurred on Memorial Day weekend in 1988, when a sudden, unseasonable storm disrupted boat transportation and stranded thousands of day visitors on the island overnight. With all hotels full, many found shelter in the local churches and school gymnasium, while 1200 spent the night sitting in Avalon Theatre. Their host, the Santa Catalina Island Company, provided free beverages and snacks.

On the level between the theater and mezzanine are the projection room, storage areas, and a fitness center. Cloak rooms and restrooms are on the mezzanine, a fortunate location for traffic flow—keeping the crowds around such facilities away from the ballroom floor. Above the ballroom is a huge attic that houses ballroom ventilation equipment.

The ballroom and theater ventilation systems are separate. Air in either area can be changed in three to four minutes. To heat both areas, steam heat and hot water were originally piped to the Casino from the Hotel St. Catherine steam plant in nearby Descanso Canyon. In 1946, after World War II, a boiler was installed on the ground floor of the building and provided heating until the early 1980s when it wore out. In the ballroom, steam radiators around the wall provided heat; in the theater, air circulation was directed through three large radiators located behind the stage. However, as the boiler had ceased to function, the radiators in both areas were removed during the 1990s renovation. The ballroom is now unheated; electrical heating is provided in the theater.

In addition to the fireproof nature of its construction materials, the building has further fire protection. From the projection room down, every level has sprinklers. There are hoses throughout the building that can reach almost any spot. The theater stage is provided with an asbestos fire curtain. Ventilation shafts from the stage to the roof can be controlled to vent smoke out of the theater in case of a fire on stage.

A number of rooms may be found on the ground level of the building below the entrance and wings. Wide, windowed arches with central doors give access to these areas. The building is also equipped with a small Otis freight elevator with stops at ground floor, mezzanine, and ballroom.

Originally, the unplastered concrete walls, still bearing their form impressions, were brush painted a light gray-white, with darker tones emphasizing details. The color was changed to cream in 1946, and the trim changed from blue-green to rose. On special occasions, flags flutter gaily over the red Catalina tile roof on 26 flagpoles encircling the balcony.

The 25 ft. lantern cupola atop the building was illuminated by a circle of neon lights before World War II. After the war's blackout, a large light bulb replaced the neon. This cupola houses the ventilation shaft for the ballroom. Also on the roof, two ventilation shafts for the theater stage face out to sea in little towers.

Three corbeled arches lead into the theater loggia, located between the two wings that house the ramps. The loggia is 40 ft. high, its interior walls decorated with nine mural panels, 10 ft. wide by 25 ft. high. Done in Art Deco style, the decor has an angular composition with a vertical emphasis and stylized decorations. A ticket booth of black marble, aluminum, and glass, 17 ft. in height, is in the center between four sets of theater doors. At each end are entrance doors to the ramps (six in each wing) that ascend on a 15% grade to the ballroom.

The loggia floor is of Catalina tile, most of which is still original and is beginning to show the wear of 70 years of happy feet. The ceiling vaults were originally of silver leaf, which eventually deteriorated. In 1994, during the restoration, the vaults were painted with a special paint containing silver. The metal grilles are of aluminum, and the five huge hanging lanterns are of bronze and frosted glass. A second ticket booth for the ballroom is located near the north ramp.

The building basks in the Catalina sun during the day—its sides a warm haven for winter swimmers—and is beautifully illuminated at night by a bank of spotlights located on the ridge above. The archways surrounding the building are lighted from below. Interior colored lighting effects in both the theater and ballroom are equally impressive.

In general, the style could be called Spanish Colonial Revival with a California flair. It has also been referred to as Mediterranean. The balcony was inspired by the columns of the Moorish Alhambra in Spain, which Mr. Wrigley admired. Rising as it does from the water, the building has also been called reminiscent of a Venetian palace or an Adriatic fortress. Yet, the massive construction does not look heavy. The eye is directed upward by the buttresses with their flaring corbeled arches, severe in contrast to the lacy detail of the balcony they support. Webber, who was noted for strong construction, and Spaulding, who was noted for light, airy effects, combined their talents well. The building is an exciting example of the imaginative integration of historical elements into a modern structure.

Architect Spaulding was particularly impressed with Mr. Wrigley's breadth of vision, not only in wanting to keep Catalina unspoiled, but also in wanting to build solid, permanent structures of architectural grace. Lamenting the modern tendency to build "grotesque towers," he praised Mr. Wrigley's efforts on Catalina to recall the gracious and generous traditions of California's early settlers."The custom in California has been to build resort buildings in a very flimsy manner, but they never are satisfactory and do not long endure," Spaulding wrote. "To avoid this mistake the Santa

Catalina Island Company has built brick plants, tile factories, rock crushers, etc., in order to provide building materials for the Island. The effect of the use of such materials is already quite obvious, for by climbing to the crest of any of the lower hills overlooking Avalon Bay one is already impressed by the red tile roofs and whitewashed walls which are reminiscent of the smaller villages of Southern Europe."[2]

The Casino was the culmination of a ten-year building program, the most monumental of William Wrigley Jr.'s efforts outside of Chicago where the Wrigley Building had already gained him fame as a builder with vision. The new Casino won an Honor Award from the American Institute of Architects, Southern California Chapter, in 1930—one of fourteen awards from a field of over 3,000 nominations for the years 1927-1930.

4   Building the Casino

David M. Renton was William Wrigley Jr.'s master builder on Catalina Island, undertaking the ten year building program that culminated in the magnificent Casino. Mr. Wrigley had many interests and, although the development of the Island was one of his major concerns, he spent but a few months a year in residence (usually when the Chicago Cubs were on the Island training). He relied heavily on his general manager to carry out Island projects and expressed his affection and confidence repeatedly in their voluminous correspondence.

David M. Renton, 1883-1947

Upon hearing that "D. M." had crawled between the floor of the ballroom and dome of the theater to see how far sound or vibration would carry when the floor was filled with dancers, Mr. Wrigley wrote: "Was amused at your going under the floor... There's nothing that gets away from you. You generally find things are going to happen before they do. Or else make sure they are not going to happen."[3]

Constructing a building of the size and complexity of the Casino on an offshore island was a considerable undertaking, but D. M. Renton had the background for the job. He had already built a hotel and cottages atop Mt. Wilson at the site of the astronomical observatory, and that project required packing materials in by mule and burro. His ability to choose and organize contractors had been further refined by his experience building tract houses (then a novel idea) in Pasadena, where he first met William Wrigley Jr. while working on the Wrigley home (now headquarters for the Tournament of Roses).

Mr. Wrigley was a good judge of character and decided that D. M. Renton was the man he needed for Catalina. When the Pasadena contractor pointed out that his business interests were already established, Mr. Wrigley told him to pack it all up and move to the Island because that was going to become his life's work. That prophecy proved true, and "D. M." had years of experience building on the Island by the time Mr. Wrigley had the idea for the Casino.

Under Mr. Renton's supervision, Santa Catalina Island Company employees began work on the site for the new building in early February of 1928. The first task was to tear down the structure already there—Sugarloaf Casino. This was completed by the end of the month, and work on the new foundations commenced in earnest, using three shifts of workmen. Newspaper reports of the time state that workmen were trying to complete the building in time for the summer season, and estimated the cost at $600,000. Both estimates were subsequently revised.

Using a gas shovel wherever possible, construction crews dug to bedrock (40 feet down in some cases), sank shafts and laid floors of 10 in. timber, then poured about eight tons of concrete into each one. Settling of only 1/8 to 3/4 of an inch was proudly reported. During this time, a runway was built around the north side of the site, from which building supplies could be deposited by trucks at convenient points. Transportation Department head Johnny Windle was kept particularly busy during the ensuing year.

CIM Collection

Pouring the foundations, April 12, 1928

The foundations were completed by early May, and Llewellyn Iron Works of Los Angeles erected two large guy derricks on the site for handling steel girders. Operated by electric power, these cranes had 110 ft. masts, 100 ft. booms, and lifted a 20 ton load. Each night at least a barge load of

The Casino

Erecting the derrick, April 26, 1928

building material was towed across the channel and unloaded at the site. At some time several barges would be anchored off the rock quarry waiting their turn.

The steel structural work was completed by the end of June. In photographs at this phase, the Casino looks like the effort of a child genius with a giant erector set. D. M. Renton, who had high respect for efficiency and on-the-job rapport, was quick to express his appreciation in a letter to his friend, David Llewellyn, which read in part:

Steel framing for ballroom, June 1, 1928

"It certainly has been a pleasure to work and cooperate with such a force of engineers and workmen that your good firm had on this building. They are a jovial crew, and in that frame of mind it is easy to discern that they are satisfied in every respect, and all endeavored to exert every effort to complete the work efficiently and at the earliest possible date...

"One of the items which impressed me forcibly was the fact that out of a great many pieces of steel going into this building they all dovetailed in nicely; no errors or delays, and everything was perfected in the shop before being delivered on the job."[4] In all, there were 28,222 pieces of shapes and plates installed.

The reinforced concrete walls came next. With the help of the derricks,

The Casino with Surarloaf Rock, June 25, 1928

concrete was poured in place, rising slowly up the building frame. Another derrick on the freight pier unloaded the barges and immediately transferred the material to the building. Over 500 employees were reportedly working in the various construction departments at this time. Skilled men were brought from the mainland; many others were hired locally. The top story of the building was completed in August. By then, the opening date was projected to the following season, and cost estimates had reportedly risen to $1,000,000.

Catalina Clay Products, the tile plant, had been rapidly turning out brick and tile for the building, using native clay. Plumbing, ventilation, and electrical contractors all had their complicated installation tasks. Moving through this beehive of activity, consulting with the architects and engineers and keeping an eagle eye on everything, was D. M. Renton, enjoying himself immensely. He had assembled at least sixty different contractors and their crews. Scheduling was tight and coordination was extremely important. Each contractor's crew and the materials and equipment they needed had to arrive on the Island in proper sequence if the work was to proceed without delay.

With winter storms approaching, attention was given to reinforcing the Point with rock from the adjacent beaches. This task the Santa Catalina Island Company accomplished, using its own tugboat and barge. When Sugarloaf Rock was blasted away in March, the debris was used for further reinforcement. Newspaper reports now estimated the costs at $1,500,000. William Wrigley Jr. and a party of friends toured the building early in February to make a last check on its progress. Mr. Wrigley then left the Island but kept in close touch with "D. M." by letter. On occasions warranting the use of that novel new instrument at Catalina, the telephone, he would send a telegram ahead to announce the time of his call.

The Casino

Final stages of construction, March 1929

Decoration of the interior had begun about the first of the year, and artists were soon scrambling around on scaffolding while workmen added other finishing touches to the building. The grounds were cleared and the road from Avalon—dubbed Casino Way—was widened during March and April. By then artists were working day and night. Technicians had installed the Page Organ in the theater and were adjusting it. On April 24, Philip K. Wrigley and a party of family and friends were given an inspection tour of the building by D. M. Renton.

In the theater, all of the lights were turned on, to murmurs of appreciative amazement, and the organ was demonstrated. When the group reached the ballroom, they were treated to the rhythms of an impromptu orchestra composed of Harry Brantford (saxophone), Githart Hansen (banjo), Benny Ogden (drums), and Arthur Renton (guitar and voice). The acoustics, in the empty ballroom, seemed fine. Arthur, Mr. Renton's youngest son, had also conducted an earlier test, to the great amusement of the workmen, when he drove his red Model T Ford runabout up the ramp to the ballroom.

The official opening was announced—Wednesday, May 29, 1929. Gardeners placed a row of palm trees along the Descanso side of the point and planted flowers and shrubs to complete the landscaping. Mrs. Wrigley's flower garden had been sacrificed to the exigencies of the day. Estimated costs had risen to $2,000,000. Alma Overholt, Mr. Wrigley's publicist for the Island, wrote rapturous newspaper articles describing the decor and capacities of the new "pleasure palace." Her paeans of praise now seem flowery, but the fact remains that a unique and beautiful building had been erected on Sugarloaf Point.

Islanders and their friends were invited to preview the building on

May 25th. It was under their dancing feet that D. M. Renton made his final inspection tour, crawling between the floors. No doubt he breathed a sigh of relief that the building was finally completed. The use of cantilever construction for such a structure was new, as was the idea of a building with the ballroom on top and the theater below. He was certainly justified if he also felt some pride in his accomplishment.

Mr. Renton had high standards and great energy. He expected good performance from the men who worked for him, and he picked them well. He was also a hearty, outgoing man, who valued a cooperative, pleasant working atmosphere and rewarded work well done. Typically, during the opening ceremonies of the Casino, he praised at length the efforts of all the men who had worked on the building. The wild ovation he received in return testified to his personality and achievement.

Mr. Wrigley's praise had come earlier. When being congratulated for his improvements to the Island, Mr. Wrigley had proclaimed publicly: "Don't forget that to Mr. Renton should go the credit for building into realities the things that have been accomplished here. I come out here twice a year and give instructions for a flock of new ideas to be carried out. But it is Mr. Renton who supplies my hands and actually does the job, and always has it finished ahead of time."[5]

William Wrigley Jr. and D. M. Renton formed a rare and happy combination of talents, much to the lasting benefit of Santa Catalina Island. The Casino is a spectacular tribute to their efforts.

CIM Collection

William Wrigley Jr. and D. Renton at the Catalina Visitors Country Club

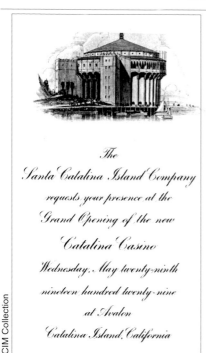

The
Santa Catalina Island Company
requests your presence at the
Grand Opening of the new
Catalina Casino
Wednesday, May twenty-ninth
nineteen hundred twenty-nine
at Avalon
Catalina Island, California

CIM Collection

5 Opening Ceremonies

For the gala opening of the new Casino, the City of Avalon proclaimed a legal holiday starting at noon on Wednesday, May 29, 1929, and requested all places of business to close. Flags were draped across the street and hung from building fronts along Crescent Avenue. Multi-colored tricorners flew from the poles encircling the Casino roof and were strung in ropes along with American flags from the entrance to the banks of the adjacent hill.

Engraved invitations to the opening had been sent to a selected list of guests. The cover bore a colored drawing of a pirate lass (sporting a Wrigley banner on her cockade hat) directing her mate to open a large "pleasure chest"—the theme of the opening ceremony. A general invitation to the public had been issued in the newspaper. A special evening sailing of the steamer from Wilmington was scheduled to return early Thursday morning, but, in general, people were planning on a four day weekend. Festivities began with a parade along Crescent Avenue to the Casino when the South Pasadena Drum and Bugle Corps arrived on the noon steamer.

CIM Collection

A glowing account of the day's activities, presumably by Alma Overholt, appeared in the local newspaper, as follows:

The Flag Raising

"One of the most beautiful and impressive flag raising ceremonies marked the beginning of the colorful opening program of the magnificent new Catalina Casino Wednesday, May 29. Their helmets glistening in the afternoon sun and uniforms the hue of the sea that formed their background, the sixty piece championship South Pasadena drum and bugle corps stood in formation on Sugarloaf Point, flanked by [American Legion] Catalina Post 137, the Avalon Band and Avalon and Camp Toyon Troops of Boy Scouts. To Life Scout Jack, fell the honor to unfurl Old Glory from the great flagpole. Martial music and the inspiring address given by District Attorney Buron Fitts, who flew over from the mainland for the event, filled every heart with the consciousness of the triumph of achievement. At the close, every eye turned to the beautiful building, rising as a monument to the effort of William Wrigley Jr. to give to Catalina the finest and best the world's artisans have to offer - the crowning jewel of a ten years' development program.

CIM Collection

King Neptune arrives with the key to open the New Casino

Neptune Arrives

'Taps' and the whir of a motor, and out from the horizon came the seaplane of Western Air Express, and onto the float anchored at Sugarloaf Point stepped Father Neptune, accompanied by six picturesque pirate lassies

30

lugging a rusty pirate chest brought from the depth of his domain. With merry shouting it was brought ashore but not until Father Neptune [Neal Warrick] and his retinue had faced a battery of cameras, as formidable as any world celebrity of terra firma has ever withstood, for a tripod or graflex from every 'news' and 'still' service was perched on the jagged cliffs of the Casino promontory to grind film that is to tell the world of the new Catalina.

A Surprise

"With merry shouting and followed by the great throng which attended the opening ceremonies, the chest was brought to the Casino entrance and Mr. D. M. Renton, general manager of [the SCI Co.], was presented with the golden key that lay within and bidden to open the doors of Catalina's great 'Pleasure Chest,' the Catalina Casino itself.

"Out came a 'surprise' that took the vast audience, as well as Mr. Renton, off their feet—a beautiful treasure chest wrought of white carnations, sweet peas and maidenhair fern, was brought from the Casino foyer by the pirate king and his wife [Toby Baker and Lois Harrison]. Gently the lid was opened and among a mass of golden blooms rose the most adorable little maid, just sleepily rubbing her eyes, and then waving her little arms in welcome. Across her chest, lettered on a shimmering little garment of white silk, was 'Miss Catalina.' Eagerly cameras clicked as little Miss Catalina [Claudia Clemens] was lifted from out of the chest and placed in the arms of Mr. Renton. The tableau most exquisitely carried out the motif of the beautiful invitations that had been sent out for the Casino Opening.

"The floral treasure chest was the gift of the merchants and business men of Avalon to Mr. Wrigley...

CIM Collection

Little Miss Catalina Attracts the photographers

Fashion Revue

"From the doors of the Casino the scene shifted to another treasure chest tableau, the Catalina Fashion revue on Avalon boardwalk. A huge treasure chest had been built at 'North Beach,' from out of which stepped the various activities of Catalina garbed in the proper attire for the sports they represented. Miss Tyreen Crouch depicted the Spirit of Catalina, followed by the golf girl, the tennis girl, the hiking girl, the equestrienne, the aviatrix, the yachting girl, the motor-boating girl, the huntress, the swimmer and the fisherette, a faithful reproduction of the attractive new Catalina folder with its combination 'pleasure chest' motif.

"Catalina girls who participated in the Fashion revue were Mrs. Lucile Sook... Miss Lois Harrison... Miss Mary Conrad... Miss Helen Sweney... Miss Loretta Sullivan... Miss Alfa Mattson... and Miss Barbara LeVitt, [who also] directed the costuming of the island girls and deserves much credit for both her artistic conception and ability of execution... The natty costumes worn were loaned through the courtesy of Mr. McMillan of the Avalon Dry Goods Company...

CIM Collection

Catalina sporting fashions of 1929

32

The Ballroom

"During the afternoon the El Patio-Catalina Orchestra under direction of Mr. Maurice Menge, played in the beautiful new Casino ballroom, while thousands of visitors were escorted through the building on an inspection tour by members of the entertainment committee…

"The following Avalon ladies acted as hostesses for the occasion: Mrs. D. M. Renton, Miss Sara Wrigley, Mrs. M. S. Patrick, Mrs. R. Douglas, Mrs. J. Dickenson, Mrs. P. Randall, Mrs. F. B. LeVitt, Mrs. M. A. Runyon, Mrs. T. M. Polhamus, Mrs. Ed W. Smith, Mrs. M. B. Dunkle and Mrs. S. E. Carpenter.

Many Floral Tributes

"Floral tributes from friends and business associates filled the foyer, the ramps, mid-floors, ballroom lobby and the ballroom itself, in gorgeous array. Every nook and cranny of the great building was literally banked with gorgeous blooms. Among the many beautiful pieces were the floral treasure chest, the Wrigley banner from the 'girls and boys of the Traffic Department,' crossed bats and baseball from the 'Angels,' a cushion from Harry Diffin, and hundreds of baskets, one more beautiful than the other.

Opening of Theater

"Astounded as visitors were at the magnificence of the building during the afternoon, their amazement turned almost to unbelief when the theater doors were thrown open in the evening and they were ushered into the luxurious elegance of Catalina's new pleasure palace. At each glass door entrance stood a nattily uniformed colored boy in royal blue and Spanish red, the color notes of the theater. Quaintly garbed usherettes in Spanish peasant costumes, also in blue and red with white vestees, stood at attention in each theater aisle…

From the stage, Mr. Renton read a telegram from Mr. Wrigley, then said: 'On behalf of William Wrigley, Jr., J. H. Patrick and the Santa Catalina Island Company, I welcome you to this grand opening. We hope that you will enjoy yourselves tonight as you inspect this new two million dollar theater and ballroom.' He went on to praise Mr. Wrigley as one of the world's greatest builders, to talk about the construction facts of the building, and to thank the workmen who made the building possible, as well as architects Webber and Spaulding. Alma Overholt reports that "cheer after cheer went up from the vast audience, for the man who has lived the laying of every piece of tile, the erection of each bit of steel, and the designing of every detail of the beautiful edifice, yet who modestly refuses to take any credit to himself." The newspaper account continues:

"A prelude of lighting effects and concert by the El Patio-Catalina Orchestra held the packed house spell-bound in its seats, as the beauty of the magnificent theater auditorium was absorbed.

"Avalon Town, composed by Mr. Herbert Nacio Brown, was sung by Edward Jardon, the golden throated tenor of the El Patio-Catalina Orchestra, followed by *Catalina,* an exquisite lyric written by Mrs. David M. Renton, played by the orchestra.

"A Kovert Hollywood Revue, featuring fifteen Orpheum headliners, was presented by Norman Manning, who directed the entertainment features of the opening, in a prologue of Nautch, Spanish and jazz dances, climaxed by a spectacular 'Jewel Dance.' The Hotel St. Catherine Orchestra accompanied the prologue numbers.

"A soft prelude played on the magnificent four manual Page organ with L. H. Clark at the console, marked the rising of the curtain on *The Iron Mask,* a Douglas Fairbanks production.

"Beautiful vocal duets sung by Jean Winslow, son of Admiral Winslow of the Paris Opera, and Maxine Dalglish, formerly of the Los Angeles Opera Company, gave the audience a splendid conception of the remarkable acoustics of the Casino theater auditorium, the first to have been built for the new art of the vocal screen…

"In the ballroom above the theater visitors were transported to a veritable fairyland scene. Strains of soft music played by the El Patio-

Catalina Orchestra, with Maurice Menge at the baton, came from a silver shell over which played a myriad of opalescent lights mingled with color harmonies, such as but dreams of childhood conjure. On the cork cushioned dance floor swayed several thousand couples to the rhythm of the opening dance.

"Mr. Renton extended greetings to the guests from Mr. Wrigley and dedicated the ballroom to the thousands of visitors who are to come to the new Catalina to enjoy its recreations and facilities for happy entertainment.

"The opening of the Catalina Casino will ever remain as a memorable occasion in the memory of those who were fortunate enough to have been in attendance, and marks a new epoch for Catalina, as the Play Isle, not only of the Pacific, but of the world."[6]

Newspaper accounts failed to mention the fact that the new projection equipment damaged part of the Douglas Fairbanks film, or that the acoustics of the ballroom behaved differently when it was crowded with people. Most of the local people who attended now recall only the gay confusion of the event, but theater manager Art LaShelle recalled the difficulties with the film. Orchestra members Jack Baptiste, Maury Paul, and Lank Menge (brother of band leader Maurice) remembered the complaints of dancers confused by an echoing beat, a condition that acoustical engineers remedied to a large degree within a month.

The next day, Memorial Day, the American Legion assembled another elaborate parade that included a 35 piece Mexican Band from Corona, which had played for a dance in the Mexican hall the night before. The paraders again marched to the Casino, where appropriate services featuring the El Patio-Catalina Orchestra and soloists of the previous day, along with local community groups, were held in the new Avalon Theatre.

Many yachts joined in a marine parade led by Vice Commander Pabst of the Catalina Island Yacht Club to escort the ketch *Nomad* on her departure on a five year voyage around the world. D. M. Renton had presented the boat's owners, Stephens Miranda and Daniel Blum, with a log for their journey the day before. As on the previous day, water sports continued in the bay.

The newspaper reported an estimated 10,000 people in Avalon during the two days of ceremonies. Visitors inspected the new edifice on both days. The Casino was declared a huge success, and the town settled down to pleasure as usual, with the new theater and ballroom attracting record crowds to the Island.

50th Anniversary Celebration

Fifty years later, on May 29, 1979, a new generation of the Pasadena High School Marching Band marched along Crescent Avenue to the Casino. Father Neptune and his pirate lassies again presented their pirate chest, and the granddaughter of the original "adorable little maid" stepped forth in a reenactment of the opening ceremonies of the now historic building.

The 50th anniversary festivities were organized by Charles M. Liddell (owner) and William W. Bushing (general manager) of Catalina Island Odyssey, who took great care to recreate the original event as closely as possible. An extensive search had turned up descendents of original participants and, on occasion, the originals themselves. Thus, the child Claudia Mysel stepped forth from the pleasure chest while her grandmother looked on.

In the packed theater, master of ceremonies Carl Bailey, "Mr. Big" of radio station KBIG, introduced representatives of the Santa Catalina Island Company, including Malcolm Renton, son of Casino builder D. M. Renton, and Paxson Offield, grandson of William Wrigley Jr. Also acknowledged were Richard Webber, son of Walter Webber of the original architectural firm of Webber and Spaulding; Mrs. Sally France, daughter of chief designer Rowland Crawford; Mrs. Fred Paulson, wife of Avalon's mayor who led the parade in 1929; and members of various Big Bands who had played in the historic ballroom. Celebrities in attendance were film and television actor Gregory Harrison (a native son) and musician Doodles Weaver (who had a long association with the Island).

Many celebrities sent telegrams of congratulation. One, in particular, struck a responsive chord in the hearts of the audience. It came from John

Wayne, who had made Catalina a favorite getaway since his youth. Wayne, who died of cancer less than a month later, had reluctantly declined to be master of ceremonies. By letter, he reminisced about Sugarloaf rock where the Casino now stands, staying at the Island Villas, and band concerts under the stars, commenting "and boy that's a year or two ago".

California State Assemblyman Gerald Felando presented the Santa Catalina Island Company with a special commendation from the legislature in Sacramento. Jim Pulliam, president of the Southern California Chapter of the American Institute of Architects, bestowed a duplicate of the original award the building received from the American Institute of Architects on March 28, 1930. Again repeating history, William Wrigley did not attend the celebration but sent his best wishes, as had his grandfather William Wrigley Jr. before him.

Master of Ceremonies Carl Bailey escorted the audience down memory lane, remembering events from 1929 when talkies were new, the stock market had not crashed, and bread was 10 cents a loaf. He then introduced Jeannie Hill, who served as fashion commentator for a review of 1929 fashions for the active Catalina woman. To the audience's delight, Jeannie, whose mother Lucile Sook had modeled in the original fashion show (and was sitting in the audience watching her daughter model her original costume), introduced a bevy of local beauties wearing outfits recreated from photographs of the original show. A slide show of the construction of the Casino followed, along with entertainment by Bombi the Clown.

Gaylord Carter, one of the nation's best known theater organists, then played a medley of popular songs on the Page Organ, including music written about Catalina over the years, which he arranged using sheet music from the Catalina Island Museum archives. Next, local organist Robert D. Salisbury took a turn at the Page to accompany the Avalon Community Chorus in a medley of Catalina songs.

The final treat of the afternoon was the Douglas Fairbanks Sr. film, *The Man in the Iron Mask*. This movie had not actually been seen at the original opening because the projection equipment had eaten the film, so some of the audience had been waiting 50 years to see it. The film, a transition between silent and talkie, originally had a musical sound component with Fairbanks the only actor speaking and then only during the second half. The original sound component had deteriorated and the actor's son, Douglas Fairbanks Jr., released it for screening only after he had provided a new sound track on which he voiced his father's speaking parts. The print was excellent and the audience was charmed.

Although the 50th anniversary celebration successfully carried the participants back in time, not all of the original events could be recreated. There was no big band dance in the Casino ballroom. Musical tastes had changed and visitors were not particularly interested in ballroom dancing on Memorial Day weekend; other amusements claimed their attention. But for history buffs, the 50th anniversary of the Casino brought back a host of pleasant memories.

6 Avalon Theatre

Theatergoers passing through the glass doors lettered in gold "Avalon Theatre" find themselves in a foyer paneled in black walnut to a height of 12 feet under a beamed barrel ceiling of coral-red shot with golden stars. The ceiling beams are black, rimmed with bands of silver and peacock blue. Alternating among the beams are lighting fixtures and painted ornamentation in sunburst patterns. The 25 ft. wide foyer is 160 feet long, curved in the arc of a circle. Men's and women's restrooms located on opposite sides of the foyer are decorated with original Catalina tile.

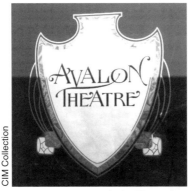

Avalon Theatre logo

A black onyx drinking fountain graced the foyer until 1994, when it was removed during the renovation because of the water damage it was causing to the historic black walnut paneling. Drinks are still available at the popcorn, candy and soft drink counter installed in 1949 when refreshments were first allowed in the theater. The four torchieres, replacing the original standing lamps, and four table lamps date from the 1994 renovation, as do the light fixtures in the women's restroom.

Red carpeting with a blue and gold floral design covers the foyer and auditorium. This is new carpeting, with a design similar to the original, installed during the 1994 renovation. The original covering in the middle sections of both the foyer and theater had to be replaced in 1966. Now the only piece of original carpeting remaining is located in a small room near the candy counter.

The original foyer furniture, made in the Catalina Furniture Factory, was designed in a futuristic style and brightly colored in keeping with the modernistic decor of the interior. It reportedly included benches, tables, chests, and high-backed settees, some pieces of

Avalon Theatre lobby, 1929

which now grace the chorus dressing room off the theater foyer. This foyer furniture was replaced in 1941 under the direction of Mrs. Philip K. Wrigley, who was involved at the time in the redecoration of the Atwater Hotel and other Island properties. The overstuffed sofas now in place date from that time. They were re-upholstered in 1994.

Numbered Art Deco aisle signs in black glass and bronze mark the three auditorium entrances hung with double curtains. The outer draperies

Panorama of the theater murals

were originally of orange-vermilion damask decorated with silver, curvilinear, floral designs. The inner ones had a jagged stripe design. Both sets of draperies were later changed to beige and lined with black. The current draperies, hung during the 1994 renovation, are blue with gold detail.

Once through the curtains, the theatergoer finds himself at the rear of the auditorium under the three coves of the projection room. Before him is a circular domed space shaped like a giant inverted coconut and unbroken by pillars or balconies. It is 138 feet across and 43 feet high. Overhead, star designs decorate a ceiling made of hard acoustical material originally covered with silver leaf. During the 1994 renovation, the deteriorated silver leaf was replaced with a custom paint containing silver. Lights recessed behind star-shaped openings also twinkle in the ceiling. Scaffolding was hung through these openings during construction.

Murals decorate the base of the dome above 7 ft. wall panels of rose colored acoustical material trimmed in black. A 44 ft. wide and 24 ft. high proscenium arch defines the stage, which is revealed when the movie screen is raised. The stage was state-of-the-art when the building was built in

Panorama of the theater murals

41

Panorama of stage area

1929 and was suitable for live theater productions. Since then, however, technological innovations in set design have rendered the compact space inadequate for most modern staging. In 1953, the original movie screen was replaced by a wider screen (20 ft. high and 37 ft. wide) to accommodate cinema scope. In 1989, this screen was replaced by a new "fly away" screen, which can be raised so that the stage can be used. In the orchestra pit in front of the stage, on the left, is the gilded console of a four-manual Page Theatre Organ installed when the theater was first built. (The orchestra pit had been covered in 1941 for a stage production and so remained until the 1994 renovation.)

On each side of the proscenium arch, mounted on an eight-sided shaft of basalt, is a flame-like figure of a boy on a dolphin, painted vermilion. Above the three theater entrances are mounted large pairs of rectangular plaques bearing the laughing and weeping faces of "comedy" and "tragedy" in relief. These and the single masques over each of the four exits have an Oriental flavor.

The original seating capacity of the theater was 1250 (although through some error a figure of 2500 was given in early publicity), but the first two rows of seats were found to be too close to the screen and were soon removed. During the 1994 renovation, another 20 seats were removed, leaving a present capacity to seat 1164 persons.

During the 1994 renovation, all of the theater seats were dismantled (and carefully numbered for return to their original location) so that the flooring could be refinished. The original iron bases, of a Spanish design in red, black, and gold, were then carefully cleaned. The seats were reupholstered in red velvet, including the ten rows of more elaborate wing-backed seats at the rear of the auditorium that constitute the loge. The original upholstering was red velvet as well, although that on the general admission seats had a chevron design.

View from stage to projection booth

The projection room above the entrance aisles houses a Century Optical Reproducer Head using Zenon light. Film is fed to this projection unit by a platter. This projection equipment with its computerized power source was installed in 1990, along with Dolby Surround sound, and is comparable to that in the average theater on the mainland. This equipment replaced two Brenkert 35mm projectors with two Brenkert carbon arc lights, which had been in use since 1939 and are still used when showing early silent films (which can be easily damaged by the newer equipment). Prior to

1939, two Model E7 Simplex projectors and a Model 6B Powers (for newsreels and special shorts) were used. This original equipment, along with an original Brenkert, combined-effect, slide and floodlight projector (commonly called a stereopticon) for creating lighting effects on the proscenium arch, remains in the projection room as well, creating a mini-museum of historic projection equipment. Other lighting effects, controlled either from the projection room or a switchboard in the foyer, are achieved by regulating the banks of lights (in four colors) concealed behind the theater wall.

1939 Brenkert 35mm projectors with carbon arc lights still used for showing silent films

Avalon Theatre was one of the first designed for sound to accommodate the new "talkies" ushered in with the release of *The Jazz Singer* in 1927, featuring Al Jolson. (Jolson, by the way, sang as a young man at Catalina and was involved in the writing of the song *Avalon* along with Vincent Rose and Billy de Silva.) During construction, consulting acoustical engineers Dr. F. R. Watson of the University of Illinois and Prof. Vern 0. Knudson of the University of California, Southern Branch (now UCLA) worked with the architects and decorator to produce excellent acoustics in the new theater.

Basically, sounds rise to the ceiling and flow equally down the surface of the dome to all parts of the auditorium. The murals around the base of the dome conceal a six inch layer of hair felt cloth set on a wooden framework. This is covered by a light dust cloth. Stretched over this and mitered into the hard ceiling shell is the fabric on which the murals are painted. This arrangement of materials absorbs the sound to prevent reverberations. Of course, there is one magic spot—right in the center of the theater—where the stamp of a foot will produce an echo that may bounce up to fifteen times from ceiling to floor and back.

At the time it was built, the theater was received warmly by movie producers and directors who were busily experimenting with sound (and shooting many of their films on the Island). Producer William De Mille commented to D. M. Renton after testing the theater's acoustics, "It is amazing that William Wrigley, Jr., who is not a theatrical man, should be the first man to have built the theater we have been praying for. The credit for this achievement alone will be worth all the effort and great expense. Mr. Wrigley has done what every producer of sound pictures has been hoping could be done. The Catalina Casino is the first theater auditorium that has been built for sound pictures and in my tests I have found it to be absolutely perfect in its acoustics."[7]

In 1931, when Radio City Music Hall in New York City was being built, engineers involved in that project traveled to the Island to study the acoustics of Avalon Theatre. The Radio City auditorium was subsequently designed along the same line, with the addition of balconies.

The Murals

The distinctive murals of Avalon Theatre created by John Gabriel Beckman are a feature which leave a lasting impression on visitors. Gabriel Beckman was a well-known young artist with a number of theaters to his credit, including Grauman's Chinese Theatre in Hollywood, when D. M. Renton introduced him to William Wrigley Jr. in Pasadena. After seeing a sketch prepared on two days' notice, Mr. Wrigley hired

CIM Collection

John Gabriel Beckman

Beckman to do the murals for the Casino. Work had already started on the site and Beckman quickly began to work on his designs in earnest.

By the time the theater was ready for decoration, Beckman's design had evolved from its original Greek theme to reflect the underwater surroundings of the new Casino and local historical and landscape motifs.

CIM Collection

Original working sketch of theatre mural During three months of intensive work,

45

Original sketch of theatre mural

Beckman and a team of artists worked day and night to execute the murals in time for the grand opening. This task completed to everyone's satisfaction, the artist went on to other waiting commitments.

The Stock Market Crash in November of 1929 and subsequent depression brought to a sudden stop a number of Beckman's projects, including a proposed Los Angeles Country Club. The bottom had dropped out of the mural market, and the young artist, looking elsewhere for work, found a place in the movie industry as a set designer. About this time he began to go by the name of John rather than Gabriel. The Island lost touch with him completely.

By serendipitous coincidence, when the Catalina Island Museum Society was beginning its research in 1978 for the original edition of this book, a young man visiting the museum casually mentioned that his "boss" had painted the theater murals. Following this lead, the Society was delighted to discover that John Gabriel Beckman was not only alive and well but actively working as an art director for Columbia Studios. He was invited to the Island where he saw his murals for the first time in almost 50 years—

Casino entrance

proving untrue a report he had heard years earlier that they had been painted over. He spent many hours reminiscing and answering questions about the execution of the murals.

The first series of Beckman murals the theatergoer sees are nine huge panels on the walls of the entrance loggia. These are underwater scenes of colorful stylized marine life floating against a green background. Mr. Wrigley had asked him if he could do underwater scenes, and Beckman recalls making daily trips around Sugarloaf Point in a glass bottom rowboat to draw inspiration from nature while designing these panels.

Such excursions were not only enjoyable but also successful, for although the fish, starfish, jellyfish, and other marine life depicted are quite fantastic, the total effect is that of life deep in a watery forest of kelp—life complete with a sinuous mermaid, who floats in the central panel.

The murals were designed to be executed in glazed Catalina tile. In the rush to complete the building, however, this plan was abandoned, and the scenes were painted directly onto the concrete surface. They are exposed to the weather and afternoon sun and have had to be touched up several times, most

Casino entrance mural

Casino entrance mural

Mermaid mural

recently for the occasion of the Casino's 50th anniversary. This delicate task was always entrusted to local artist Roger M. Upton Sr., and later to Roger M. Upton Jr.

Visitors will notice that the central mural over the box office differs from the others. It is now executed in tile, a direct result of the Island's rediscovery of John Gabriel Beckman. After conversations with the artist and ceramicist Richard Keit of RTK, Inc., the Santa Catalina Island Company decided to redo the mermaid mural in tile as originally planned, at a cost of over $35,000.

Beckman worked with Keit to recreate the original colors as closely as possible and the artist attended a grand unveiling of the new mural on July 19, 1986. The original design had called for wavy edged tile, but this proved too difficult to execute and square tile were substituted. Beckman had originally conceived of the mermaid as having more brightly red hair. The overall effect of the new mural is more subdued than originally intended but Beckman himself had mellowed over the years and declared that he was well pleased with the more subtle effect.

The murals in the theater auditorium were painted on a form of jute material, like burlap. For color, "11 grind" pigments were used (that's a finer grind than the well-known Windsor & Newton artist colors) in a medium of flatene, a binder used by printers to bind ink to paper. The bright true colors were softened somewhat by the jute material but also mellowed with

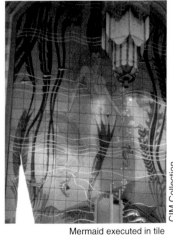

Mermaid executed in tile

CIM Collection

Mural detail, Spanish ships and friars motif

time and accumulated dust. To everyone's delight, the colors were brought out again through the efforts of a trained art conservator during the 1994 renovation. (See Mural Restoration, p. 53) The jute material stretches from the base of the dome in triangular shapes, the straight seams being disguised by scalloped lines in the design.

From the rear of the theater, the motion of the murals carries the eye around each side of the dome toward the culmination of the total design in the proscenium arch. On the left, the sequence of motifs includes exotic birds and flowers, a Spanish ship, hooded friars, and an archer aiming at a fleeing deer. On the right, the sequence features cactus and succulents, leaping goats, exotic foliage, and Indians astride charging horses. (To give an example of scale, the horses are 16 feet long.) At the rear of the theater, the exotic scenery includes incredible birds and flowers, a waterfall, and two elegant monkeys.

The motifs were suggested by Southern California scenery and history but, according to Beckman, are not meant to tell a story or depict actual events. On each side, five abstract design elements of wavelike shapes rise to peaks above the figure motifs, echoing the underwater quality achieved

Mural detail, Indians and horses motif

by the mural panels in the theater loggia. The overall effect is of great vitality and movement among the stylized figures and shapes. At the time, Beckman's work was dubbed futuristic and was praised for its felicitous blend of the classic and modern and for being dramatic and startling but not extreme. Now, the murals are often referred to as an example of Art Deco style.

To each side above the proscenium arch is a mass of gilded grillwork shaped in stylized, overlapping disks, giving the effect of clouds and concealing the pipes of the theater organ. In the center is a figure of Venus rising from the waves on a seashell (after Botticelli) borne by seahorses and the figures of Triton and Neptune. This culminating figure of the murals is painted to give the illusion of relief, which is enhanced by spotlighting from the orchestra pit below.

Within the proscenium arch, a fleet male figure and his shadow-like backward looking twin stride with arms outstretched on the crests of giant waves across an asbestos fire curtain. The background (etched against 22 karat gold leaf) is a topographic map of Catalina Island, including latitude and longitude. These swift figures were described in the original publicity as depicting "The Flight of Fancy Westward" and as being symbolic of William Wrigley Jr.'s movement across the country from the East, first to Chicago then to California. They were also said to be symbolic of "Catalina on the go."

Mr. Wrigley's rise to fame and fortune was spectacular and rapid. He was a man who liked to get things done, an attribute shared by D. M. Renton and reflected in the rapidity with which the Casino was built. The building was scheduled to be completed on May 24th and time was fast running out when it finally reached the stage where the artists could begin work on the murals.

Beckman had assembled a team of five artists—Emil Kosa Jr., Aloyous Bohnen, Vyseled Vlianoff, Eugene Goncz, and Alexander Kiss—and numerous helpers to execute the murals. The group worked on sections of giant scaffolding rigged with flood lights. Heat was used to speed the drying of the paint.

The task of coordinating this intense effort required great patience and diplomacy. Each of the major artists was accomplished in his own right and had his own ideas as well as a goodly portion of "artistic" temperament. Each artist also had his own forte, such as hands, faces, figures, flowers, or costumes, and after the basic cartoon of the mural had been transferred to the wall, each would work on appropriate sections. Beckman recalled that Kosa and Bohnen worked on the figure of Venus.

While examining the murals on his 1978 visit, Beckman searched for signatures. He couldn't remember exactly which sections each artist had executed, and was disappointed that they had not signed their work. As it turned out, he hadn't signed the work either. He obligingly remedied this oversight with a borrowed pen, while poised on a rickety box behind the wall to the left of the main auditorium entrance.

Those privileged to accompany the artist as he strode around the theater reexamining his work after so many years found the experience thoroughly enjoyable, being both instructive and amusing. He recalled that for the statuettes, the boy on a dolphin (a theme he adapted from the Greeks and

Mural detail, monkeys and exit masques

which has since become quite popular) started out as a girl. The statuettes were made by a well-known Italian sculptor (name lost) in his Los Angeles studio. Also, Beckman would have preferred the masques above the exits to be in the Greek rather than Oriental manner, but they were under the control of Rowland Crawford, the head architectural designer.

When Beckman saw the two monkeys, their black faces rimmed with white, he told of an incident that had occurred many years after the murals were painted during a visit to a zoo in Japan. There he came upon a group of monkeys whose faces were surrounded by a ruff of white fur. They looked extremely familiar. Only later did he realize that he had created them in his imagination many years before.

The Casino murals have passed the test of time. Although no longer daring or startling to the theatergoer who has experienced the incredible developments in art in the last century, they nevertheless remain intriguing. They have value not only as a historical statement, but also because of the intrinsic interest of the shapes and designs themselves. The effect is pleasing, and the entertainment continues with repeated viewing, for there is always a new figure or arrangement of shapes to discover. Beckman told us that he had always loved color and was pleased with the original effect of the murals. Upon seeing them again after almost fifty years, he exclaimed, "The effect is different... they have mellowed... but I like what I see now." So do several generations of Islanders and visitors from all over the world

Mural Restoration

The murals in Avalon Theatre were restored in 1994 as part of the general renovation of the building. John Gabriel Beckman died in 1989 at age 91 (in his sleep, after working a full day at the television studio where he was an art director) so he did not see his creation returned to its full glory, but, undoubtedly, he would have approved.

The restoration of the murals was entrusted to Eva Matysek Fine Art Restoration of Torrance, California. A trained painting conservator, Eva Matysek spent months on scaffolding high above the floor, often lying on her back, painstakingly cleaning the murals inch by inch with tiny brushes. She carefully re-adhered flakes of paint beginning to separate from the background fabric, using approved conservation adhesives. Surprisingly little touch up was required, the silver leaf details being the most deteriorated.

CIM Collection

Painters restoring the gilded grillwork concealing organ pipes above proscenium

CIM Collection

Fine Art Restorer Eva Matysek

Matysek's meticulous restoration took four months and cost $74,000 for cleaning, protection, and conservation. During the course of her work, she discovered that the original beige color of the fabric was consistently used as part of the design and that what appeared to be gray in some areas before cleaning was actually white. What had been interpreted as fading was usually the effect of accumulated dust. The two panels on either side of the proscenium had for years appeared brighter than the rest of the murals, having been painted on a harder surface that collected dust less readily. Once the adjacent mural panels painted on fabric had been cleaned, the contrast disappeared.

The conservator fastidiously adhered to the artist's original materials and concept. She augmented her own professional experience with additional research into his media and also consulted Beckman's original detailed working sketches, which his family had donated to the Catalina Island Museum. As a result, this historic artwork has been revitalized and stabilized so that it can continue to be enjoyed by generations to come.

The Page Organ

In the 1920s, no movie theater of note was complete without a pipe organ, for these magnificent instruments supplied the background music and sound effects that accompanied the motions of the figures on the silent screen. Delivery of a new organ took about a year. One of Mr. Wrigley's first concerns, therefore, when planning the new Casino was to order the construction of a full-scale theater pipe organ. This he ordered from The Page Organ Company in Lima, Ohio.

SCI Co, Collection

View of organ pipes and sound effects

News of the arrival of the Casino organ was reported in the local newspaper in April of 1929. Installation involved placing 16 ranks of pipes (with 73-85 pipes per rank) in ceiling lofts on either side of the proscenium arch and covering them with grillwork. When all was completed (at a reported cost of $40,000) the organist had at his disposal a highly unified, four-manual key desk with a bank of three curved stop rails.

Sound effects included: bass drum, cymbal, kettle drum, Chinese gong, triangle, carillon harp, xylophone, glockenspiel, orchestral bells, snare drum, tambourine, castanets, bird whistle (A & B), Chinese drum, wood block, shuffle drum, tom-tom, anvil (1 & 2), cathedral chimes (25 notes), fire bell, police siren, door bell, pistol shot, steamboat whistle, rain, surf &

wave, thunder, klaxon (auto horn), airplane motor, and telephone bell.

L H Clark, first theater organist   Mary Oswald, 1933 organist   Sherwood Mertz, singing organist 1937-37

The Casino organ was used for movie accompaniment until sound was firmly established, but it is best remembered for the concerts given before films or during the afternoons. Leonard H. Clark was the first organist for the theater. Mrs. Mary Oswald was organist in 1933. Sherwood Mertz, featured as "the singing organist" during the 1935-1937 seasons, gave very popular afternoon and evening concerts that included novelty songs and community singing. Miss Sybil Thomas was the Casino organist during 1938 and 1939.

After World War II, free afternoon concerts were resumed from 1947 to 1950 with organist Gil Evans at the console. Evans was quite popular and reportedly drew up to 600 listeners in an afternoon. He had a wide repertoire but is fondly remembered for his medleys of tunes made popular by the Big Bands, some of which he recorded on a series of records sold locally.

Gil Evans, organist, 1947-50

For several years after Gil Evans left the Island, the organ was seldom played and fell into disrepair. Then an enthusiastic young musician arrived on the scene. Robert D. Salisbury was only fifteen when he talked Tommy Clements, the theater operator, into letting him play the organ. Bob played before each movie show during the summer season from 1958 to 1964. There were two shows nightly, so he was taxied between a restaurant where he also performed and the theater to play before the second show.

Robert D. Salisbury Collection

Robert D. Salisbury, the theater's youngest organist in 1958 (age 15)

The industrious teenager also worked as the theater janitor, which entitled him to play the organ during the day. Part of keeping an organ in good repair entails playing it. This wind instrument with hundreds of valves and bellows and other moving parts needs to be exercised. With Bob playing daily and building superintendent Dale Eisenhut making minor repairs, the organ was soon back in good shape. Before long Bob attracted the attention of Helen Wrigley (Mrs. Philip K.) and was delighted to be summoned to play special concerts for this gracious lady and her friends whenever they visited the Island. Mrs. Wrigley saw to it that funds were available when the organ needed a new generator or other repairs.

When Bob left the Island to pursue his musical career, the organ again suffered from disuse, although Dr. John Gilkerson Jr., a chiropractor and amateur organist, occasionally played the instrument. He and building superintendent Eisenhut also undertook the refurbishment of some of the leather parts in the 1970s. By then the organ was almost 50 years old.

Bob Salisbury returned to Avalon in 1979 just as the community was preparing to celebrate the 50th anniversary of the Casino. He requested that the organ be tuned. This was done and the Santa Catalina Island Company established a modest budget for maintenance. The Los Angeles

Chapter of the American Theatre Organ Society (LATOS), which is interested in the preservation of theater organs, offered to undertake repairs. In the spring of 1979, six dedicated men—Harvey Heck, Gene Davis, Harold Donze, Paul Birk, Mike Ohman, and Bob Smith—spent many days replacing leather and felt parts, repairing electrical connections, and otherwise refurbishing the instrument.

As these gentlemen explained, moths, mice, and salt air corrosion are the principal enemies of the Avalon Theatre organ. High and dry in their lofts, the pipes and chests do not suffer particularly from dampness. In fact, the pipes look almost like new. These pipes, made of lead, tin, zinc, and wood, were manufactured by the Godfried Company in Germany, but the rest of the organ's parts were made in Lima, Ohio.

The Page Organ Company (1922-1935), one of numerous organ manufacturers that did not survive the double disasters of talking pictures and the Great Depression, sold its organs primarily to theaters and churches on the East Coast and in the Midwest. A commission from William Wrigley Jr. for an organ in California was a matter to boast about. The Avalon Theatre organ (4 manual, 16 rank) is above standard size, apparently the largest instrument they produced. (In the Los Angeles area, there are a couple of organs made by different manufacturers that are larger.)

Small neighborhood theaters were usually equipped with 2-manual, 6-10 rank instruments, and three small Page Organs still exist, one each in Anderson and Hedback, Indiana, and Lima, Ohio. A large (15 rank, later changed to 16) Page instrument still exists in Fort Wayne, Indiana, in excellent condition. A combined Page-Wurlitzer organ can also be found in Marietta, Pennsylvania. (Of approximately 102 organs built by the Page Organ Company between 1924 and 1929, as far as we know, only the six listed here still remain). The 16 ranks on the Avalon Page include: tuba, tibia major, clarabella, vox celeste, open diapason, clarinet, krumet, vox humana, English post horn, oboe horn, tibia minor, major violin, minor violin, stentorphone, saxophone, and kinura.

Theater organs differ considerably from church organs, the LATOS gentlemen pointed out. They're designed to play a different type of music, their tremulous, tibias, and voxes producing a "romantic," sobbing sound from the exotic reeds. The organist accompanying silent movies would work from a cue sheet and play classical mood pieces appropriate to the action of the film. If he was good, the audience would be unaware of the music. The sound effects he would usually "ad lib" according to the organ's capabilities. The theater organ is especially appropriate for overtures, marches, and romantic tunes. In the 1920s, popular song writers often used to compose their songs specifically for the organ. Nowadays, organists usually have to convert piano scores to their needs.

The men from LATOS were enthusiastic about the Avalon Theatre organ, describing it as a "great" organ, well worth their efforts at restoring it. Such work requires patience, dexterity, and dedication, for the hundreds of little pieces of leather and felt each have to be glued and assembled carefully by hand, and, as there is no blueprint, each connection has to be traced from the console to the pipes aloft. The project was a cooperative effort—the Santa Catalina Island Company providing lodgings, the men donating their time, and the Organ Society financing the rest.

In May of 1979, the historic Page Organ figured prominently in the Casino 50th Anniversary festivities. Gaylord Carter, world-renown organist active in the revival of silent film, gave a concert for the packed theater. Bob Salisbury, who happens to be a Carter protégé, was also on the program accompanying a choral group. In July, the American Theatre Organ Society brought a group of 700 of their members to the Casino for a convention that included dinner in the ballroom and screening of the silent film *Old Ironsides* in the theater, again accompanied by the legendary Gaylord Carter.

Both the Los Angeles and the San Diego Chapters of the American Theatre Organ Society continue to make annual pilgrimages to the Island to play and hear the organ, with Bob on the program. (Organists from as far away as South Africa and Australia have also visited Avalon just to hear and play the Page.)

In 1979, Bob Salisbury again became the official house organist, playing regularly for community events in addition to offering mini-concerts before the films on weekends. He also plays about three benefit concerts a

Robert D Salisbury, organist
(again) since 1979

year, a favorite being for the Avalon Lions Club, which usually attracts up to 600 people. For about five years in the 1980's, Bob was joined by his friend, concert pianist and music professor, Dr. William Teaford, for a series of well-received organ and piano concerts, the duo billing themselves as "Salisbury and Teaford Two".

In 1990, Bob played accompaniment for two Laurel & Hardy silent films, *Two Tars* and *Big Business,* during a gala 100th birthday celebration for Stan Laurel when devoted fans converged on Avalon from around the world. (The famous comedians had been frequent visitors to Avalon during the 1930s. An avid fisherman, Stan Laurel was a member of Avalon's prestigious Tuna Club. Ollie preferred golf and the duo used to play with Mr. & Mrs. Philip K. Wrigley. The games were no doubt hilarious.) In 1996, Bob succeeded Gaylord Carter as the organist for the Catalina Island Museum's annual Silent Film Benefit.

Salisbury and the Page can now be heard on CD and audio cassette. Bob's first recording, *A Page from Avalon*, features music chosen to demonstrate the range of the organ. His other recordings feature music with themes for Christmas (*Christmas Island)* and Easter (*Avalon Sunday*). These popular CD's and cassettes are available at the Catalina Island Museum Store in the Casino and are also distributed internationally.

Recording in Avalon Theatre is a bit tricky. In general, the acoustics are excellent, but a few spots in the large domed space produce echoes. The perfect recording spot for the organ turned out to be center stage, 12 feet in the air, with the microphone facing the rear of the theatre. Based on music he recorded on the Page, Bob was voted Best Amateur Theatre Organist, United States, for 1997, by the American Theatre Organ Society.

Since 1980, the organ has been receiving expert technical attention from Jim Spohn Organ Service, which has been methodically maintaining and repairing the organ. Jim Spohn is a master organ technician, having apprenticed for 23 years with a master organ builder who traveled nationwide building, installing and repairing organs. Jim visits regularly from his home in Bakersfield, California, as a guest of the Santa Catalina Island Company. He and Bob spend days working with the classic instrument to keep it in good condition. Affectionately, they are known locally as 'The Page Boys'!

In 2001, Bob retired after being associated with The Page Organ for over 40 years. To ensure that this and other organs did not get out of shape for want of regular exercise, Jim Spohn applied modern technology to design and build a computer playback system that operates the organ. This Concerto Player program, which works from a laptop computer, is hooked into the organ's electrical switching system to record key strokes, not sounds. The program can then be used to operate the electrical system and make the organ play. The organ keys themselves won't move up and down as did the keys on early player pianos but the other elements of the organ system will function just as if there were an organist at the console. Before leaving the Island, Bob recorded hundreds of songs and built a library of organ music for the future. A young organist, John Tusack, has begun learning the intricacies of the Page Organ and demonstrates the organ on Friday and Saturday nights before the movie. Time will tell if he and the organ will be long-term partners and in the meantime, Bob's presence can still be felt and heard via the new computer system.

SCI Co, Collection

Jim Spohn and Bob Salisbury

7   Theatre History

Varied forms of live dramatic and musical entertainment have delighted audiences in Avalon Theatre over the years; however, the auditorium has always been primarily a movie house. The first theatergoers—who would have paid 50¢ for general admission, 65¢ for loge seats, or 25¢ if they were children—were greeted by a manager in a tuxedo and ushered into the magnificent theater to see silent films, with an organist providing accompaniment on the versatile Page organ.

The plan had been to show "talkies" from the very beginning—the acoustics were perfect, sound equipment had been acquired, and even the emergency generator had been labeled with a warning (still visible), "Do Not Operate While Talkies Are Playing." But theater operators all over the country were experiencing the same difficulties with their new equipment as had been encountered on opening night at the Casino. In addition, sounds on the vitaphone records were extremely difficult to synchronize with the action on the film. Words came out of mouths too soon or too late, and victims fell dead before shots were fired. Virginia Renton recalled seeing *The Hunchback of Notre Dame,* unsynchronized, in Avalon Theater during its first year of operation.

Perhaps a similar experience had prompted William Wrigley Jr. to write to D. M. Renton in April of 1929, "I am not enthusiastic about having talkies in the new theater. I've never seen but one and that was enough for me. I've talked to quite a few people…they seem to be under the impression that the pictures without the talkie are much more of a hit than with them… but they may improve on them."[8]

Nevertheless, Mr. Wrigley wanted Catalina visitors to have the latest in entertainment, so developments in sound technology were followed closely and additional equipment was soon obtained. The first sound film (with the sound on the film not on a separate record) to play in the theater was *Rio Rita* in late February of 1930. On this special occasion, organist Leonard Clark gave a concert before the film.

Avalon boasted two movie theaters at this time. The smaller, 600 seat

AVALON THEATRE
Calendar of Events
Matinee Daily, 2:00 P. M.; Nightly at 7:15 and 9:05

SATURDAY, AUGUST 7—"CAPTAINS COURAGEOUS"

Freddie Bartholomew, Spencer Tracy, Lionel Barrymore and Melvyn Douglas . . . Kipling's story of a boy who was not afraid . . . America's foremost boy star in the greatest story of his career . . . Together with a Color Cartoon and Novelty . . .**Added —Sherwood Mertz at the Organ.**

SUNDAY & MONDAY, AUGUST 8-9—"EXCLUSIVE"

Fred MacMurray, Francis Farmer and Charles Ruggles . . . **She got all the news not fit to print** . . . A girl reporter beats the man she loves at his own game . . . Also a Cartoon, a Novelty and the latest Fox News. . . **In Addition—Sherwood Mertz at the organ** again presenting his original Community Singing Program.

TUESDAY, AUGUST 10—"I COVER THE WAR"

John Wayne, Owen Gaze and Don Barclay . . . An amusing melodrama of a newsreel cameraman and his adventures during an uprising in a British Asiatic possession . . . Also the latest Novelties including the latest issue of Paramount News..
IN ADDITION A SURPRISE MAJOR STUDIO FEATURE.

WEDNESDAY & THURSDAY, AUGUST 11-12—"EVER SINCE EVE"

Marion Davies, Robert Montgomery and Patsy Kelly . . . Hail, Hail the Gags Are All Here . . . and so are the screen's funniest gagsters . . . Don't Miss It! . . . Also a Comedy and Selected Novelties . . . **Added—Sherwood Mertz at the Organ.**

FRIDAY, AUGUST 13—"PUBLIC WEDDING"

Jane Wyman, William Hopper and Raymond Hatton . . . Two newcomers to the screen in a delightful comedy farce . . . Together with the latest selected short subjects . . .
* ADDED—ON THE STAGE— A REAL BONA FIDE STAGE WEDDING——Amid all the color and glamour of Old Spain Two People Will Be Joined Together In the Holy Bonds of Matrimony . . . . Don't Fail to Read the Next Issue of The Catalina Islander, for full Description of this most colorful Event, THE FIRST PUBLIC WEDDING EVER TO BE STAGED IN SUCH AN ATMOSPHERIC SURROUNDING AS THE AVALON THEATRE.

Theatre program, 1937

Riviera Theatre, located on the corner of Crescent and Clarissa, was leased to the same management. The new Avalon Theatre remained open year round (except for three winters) prior to World War II, and the Riviera opened only during the summer. To cope with the Great Depression, prices were lowered, first for week nights and matinees, then on weekends as well. From 1934 on, prices remained generally at 40, 25, and 15¢ until they rose to 55, 40, and 25¢ in 1938, where they remained until the theater was taken over by the maritime service during the war.

The double feature movie bill usually changed daily, and there were additional short subjects. Sound finally came into its own, and in 1937, new RCA "high fidelity" sound equipment was installed with Lansing speakers. Quite a few of the movies enjoyed at Avalon Theatre in these years were filmed on Catalina Island at the flourishing movie colony located at the Isthmus.

Producers and directors such as Cecil B. De Mille, Joseph Schenck, Louis B. Mayer, Samuel Goldwyn, John Ford, and Erich Von Stroheim used the theater to view the "rushes" of each day's shooting on the Island. These screenings were very private, for work in progress was closely guarded. The public, however, was often treated to special previews after the new films were completed. The arrival of the Big Bands for the summer season around Memorial Day was often celebrated with a gala premiere at the theater, including appearances by Hollywood celebrities who often sailed over on their yachts.

Live performances were also an important part of theater entertainment. The Pomona College Glee Club (with Arthur Renton among its members) gave a concert in 1933. Local organizations such as the American Legion put on benefit minstrel and variety shows and Christmas entertainments. Quite a few vaudeville acts and revues were booked from the mid-1930's on. The public was also invited to participate in amateur talent shows, such as that of Major Bowes. They also provided live applause and laughter during numerous radio shows (usually featuring Big Bands) broadcast nationwide.

The theater auditorium served as a classroom for thousands of merchant seamen during World War II. USO performers trouped across its stage to cheer up the homesick boys who crowded the auditorium or listened to the radio broadcasts. Boxing was a regular Friday night event. Band concerts were also a regular feature, and the Hollywood Canteen Symphony Orchestra gave two performances in August of 1945.

Over the years Avalon had enjoyed the offerings of a number of summer resident theatrical groups on the stage of the Riviera or at the Bandbox Theatre in El Encanto. But in August of 1946, Avalon Theatre was the scene for the first Island premiere of a stage play, *The Gentle Approach,* by John O'Dea, a project of the Theater Production Guild, starring Robert Mitchum and Jacqueline Dewit.

In general, however, since World War II, live entertainment and movie premieres have been less of a regular feature in the theater. Nevertheless, a variety of instrumental groups occasionally entertain the community and the public from the stage. California Polytechnic Institute Band performed in 1965; the Arizona State University Band, in 1971. The Los Angeles Da Camera Society, which performs chamber music in historic sites, visited Avalon in 1986 and 1987 and ensembles performed in Avalon Theatre as well as at other historic sites in town. In the 1990s, performers in the annual Jazz Trax and Blues Festivals began playing in the theater as well as the ballroom.

Premieres of movies filmed on the Island are also still occasionally shown. *Morituri,* starring Yul Brynner and Marlon Brando, premiered in 1965, and *The Glassbottom Boat,* starring Doris Day, Arthur Godfrey, and Rod Taylor, premiered in 1966. The 1986 premiere of *Catalina, A Treasure from the Past,* a film documentary narrated by Robert Graves that was produced by UCLA graduate student Danny Miller, filled the theater. The documentary explored the Island's environmental and archaeological treasures. Appropriately, the event included a concert by the Elisabeth Waldo Ensemble, which specializes in Native American and Early Californian music using authentic pre-Columbian instruments. The film was shown on television and released in video.

The Blue Men, an independent film shot mostly in Avalon and starring

Estelle Parsons, had its premiere in Avalon Theatre in 1990. To promote the film *Speed II* in 1998, a group of reviewers were brought to the Island by cruise ship to view a 20-minute synopsis of the movie as a sneak preview, then whisked away again.

CIM Collection

Promotion for movie premiere, 1966

The Avalon community, of course, has always staged events in its beloved theater. Beauty contests for Miss Catalina or the Flying Fish Queen were popular in the 1950's. The Avalon Lions Club staged a series of hilarious burlesques, *Lions A Poppin!* during the 1960's, in which they gleefully and cleverly roasted local dignitaries and citizens.

From 1976 to 1989, the annual presentation of Handel's *Messiah* by the Avalon Community Chorus (which was formed for America's Bicentennial Celebration) was an outstanding event that attracted many mainland visitors. In this highly professional production, the local chorus was augmented by mainland voices and instrumentalists. Local choral director Margaret Felkley directed the first ten productions; another local choral director, Glenn Finney, continued the tradition.

Since 1986, Avalon Schools students have entertained their proud parents and the community with an annual Winter Concert. The local school (K-12) has quadrupled in population since World War II, outgrowing the school auditorium. Since 1987, High School Graduation has been held in the theater, with Bob Salisbury doing the musical honors on the Page Organ.

Convention groups from the mainland also use the theater both for meetings and for entertainment. During the 1960s and 1970s, Lions roamed the streets of Avalon, converging on the ballroom and theater for spectacular entertainments during their annual district conferences. The theater's primary function, however, has always been as a movie venue.

Nevertheless, with the advent of television, movie crowds decreased on the Island as they did nationwide. After remaining open year round from 1946 through 1948, the theater began to close during the winter. Western Amusement Company, which operated a number of theaters on the mainland, obtained a lease on both the Avalon and Riviera Theatres in 1949. The company closed Avalon Theatre during the winter but kept the Riviera Theatre open all year until it was converted into a bowling alley in 1961. After that, Avalon Theatre showed films only on weekends during the winter until 1987 when it again opened nightly.

Tommy Clements and his wife Sally managed Avalon Theatre for Western Amusement Company (Ted Jones and later Peggy Jones, president) for 38 years and soon became an integral part of the community. After raising her daughter Mary Ann, Sally spent 20 years as a local deputy for the Los Angeles Sheriff's Department while continuing to help at the theater. Tommy's extracurricular activities were more dramatic.

Tommy had been with Ringling Bros. Circus for 15 years before switching to theater work, and shortly after his arrival in Avalon, Bombi the Clown appeared. Bombi used to get dressed in his best suit and stroll around town amusing the children and sometimes wearing a sandwich board advertising the theater. He also loved to lead parades.

Bombi had a drawing act. Around noontime, while a crowd gathered at the entrance to the steamer pier, he would set up his easel in a favorite spot. Along with "Duke" Fishman, the official steamer greeter, KBIG announcer and interviewer, Carl Bailey, and the Troubadours, he would join in a festive welcome for passengers disembarking from the Great White Steamer. In later years, a succession of little Bombis began to appear at his side as Mary Ann presented him with four grandchildren. Bombi retired in the 1970s but made a special appearance at the Casino's 50th anniversary celebration in Avalon Theatre.

The Casino

Western Amusement Company soon learned that the theater business on the Island has its own idiosyncrasies, dependent as it is on the tourist trade. Stratagems that pack theaters on the mainland don't always work in Avalon—matinees don't lure playing children off the beach, special midnight shows don't lure happy people out of nightclubs or tired families out of bed. The company could only try to provide a variety of programming for people of all ages.

In keeping with Santa Catalina Island Company policy that the Casino remain a place of family entertainment, X-rated and pornographic films, in spite of their drawing power, were never shown. Throughout its lease, Western Amusement Company provided the public with a good percentage of first run movies (G, PG, and occasionally R-rated)—some appearing even before they were widely advertised on the mainland.

Theater attendance began to increase again during the 1970s in Avalon as well as on the mainland. Good shows once again drew good crowds. *Star Wars* sold out every time it was shown in 1977. In general, nowadays, crowds of 400-to-500 people a night are considered good during July and August. By the time the Santa Catalina Island Company resumed operation of the theater in 1987, Avalon had become much more of a year round resort. Now, to the community's delight, the theater is open nightly year around, with the program changing every Friday.

CIM Collection

Early ushers and usherettes

Prices, of course, have changed over the years. Tickets were $1.00 for adults and $.35 for children when the theater reopened to the public in 1946, after World War II. They decreased to $.70 and $.25 in 1948 (TV competition), rose to $.85 and $.25 in 1951, increased gradually to $3.00 for adults and $1.50 for children by 1979, and had reached $7.50 for adults and $5 for seniors and children in 1999. (Double features, except on rare occasions, are long gone, as are cartoons, newsreels, and other short subjects.) Usherettes progressed from their original Spanish costumes through a series of brown and gold "bell-hop" style slack suits to red smocks by the early 1980's. By the 1990's, theater staff were identifiable only by small Avalon Theatre logos on their polo shirts.

Silent Film Festival

Fifty years after being totally eclipsed by talkies, silent films are currently enjoying a limited revival in Avalon as well as around the nation! *The Black Pirate,* a Douglas Fairbanks Sr. silent film that had been partially filmed at Catalina, was included in a nine-day film festival produced by Catalina Odyssey at Avalon Theatre in June of 1979. Accompaniment on the Page organ was provided by well-known theater organist Chauncey Haines. The film festival also featured a remarkable selection of classic sound films that had been filmed at least partially on the Island.

In July of that 50th anniversary year, the American Theatre Organ Society brought a large group to the historic theater to see *Old Ironsides*. At the Page Organ was the legendary Gaylord Carter. Also on hand to reminisce about the film were Charles Farrell and Esther Ralston, the stars of this classic actually filmed at Catalina in 1926. Carter performed brilliantly and the audience surged to its feet for a rousing standing ovation at the end.

Gaylord Carter, who had begun playing for silent films as a teenager, had gone on to a successful career in radio and television (and also played for the Los Angeles Lakers basketball games at The Forum). In the 1970s, his concern about the rapid loss of the great film legacy of the silent years prompted him to spearhead the revival of silent films by obtaining prints and arranging screenings, accompanying them on the organ with his own original scores. Those with long memories were delighted to see their favorite stars again. Younger generations were amazed at the sophistication and artistry of those earlier days. Soon Carter was in great demand both in the United States and abroad. Preservation efforts were given a boost and the movie studios soon realized that there was still profit in these golden oldies.

Carter composed and recorded scores for over 30 films reissued in video format for Blackhawk (now part of The Film Preservation Institute), the Harold Lloyd Company, the British Broadcasting Company, the Museum of Modern Art in New York, the Mary Pickford Company, and Paramount Studios. He was honored as Theatre Organist of the Year in 1975 and inducted into the Theatre Organists Hall of Fame. In 1994, he was again honored as Theatre Organist of the Year.

CIM Collection

Legendary theater organist Gaylord Carter

In 1988, the Catalina Island Museum Society inaugurated its annual Silent Film Benefit with Gaylord Carter at the Page Organ accompanying *Wings*, the 1928 Oscar winner starring Buddy Rogers, Richard Arlen and Clara Bow. Buddy Rogers, who had appeared in the Casino Ballroom in 1935 with his big band, The Cavaliers, made a guest appearance. Over 800 people attended and were delighted to be transported back in time as they experienced an historic film while sitting in an historic theater listening to an historic organ played by an organist who got his start during the silent film era.

Each spring since then, the Silent Film Benefit has attracted large crowds from the mainland, many people returning year after year. They have been treated to such classic feature films as *Wings, Old Ironsides, The Black Pirate, The Mark of Zorro* (Douglas Fairbanks), *The Navigator* (Buster Keaton), *Robin Hood* (Fairbanks), *Phantom of the Opera* (Lon Chaney), and *Steamboat Bill* (Keaton). The program also includes silent short subjects and cartoons.

Gaylord Carter became a firm supporter of the museum and played for the first eight benefits. This living legend suffered a stroke in 1995 at age 91, causing him to reduce his performance schedule. The following year, he shared the spotlight with his protégé, Bob Salisbury. The Museum Society selected four short comedies—*The Rink* (Chaplin), *Tillie at the Throttle* (Gloria Swanson), *One Week* (Keaton), and *Koko the Clown*—so that the two organists could spell each other. After his last engagement, Carter suffered a second stroke and retired to his cliffside home in San Pedro, from which, on a clear day, he could see Catalina.

The world lost this great organist in the fall of 2000. Solace can be taken in the knowledge that Carter mentored many other theater organists who are keeping the tradition alive and well.

Bob Salisbury has since become the organist of choice for the popular Silent Film Benefit. Salisbury learned well from his mentor and has created the scores for the Museum's films since 1996, earning his own standing ovations from delighted audiences for his accompaniment for *My Best Girl* (Mary Pickford, Buddy Rogers), *Lilac Time* (Colleen Moore, Gary Cooper), *The Thief of Bagdad* (Fairbanks, Anna May Wong), *The Sheik* and *The Son of the Sheik* (Rudolph Valentino) and *The General* (Buster Keaton).

CIM Collection

Crowds flock to the annual Silent Film Festival

NEW CASINO, NIGHT VIEW, CATALINA ISLAND, CALIFORNIA

3215-29

Postcard, 1929

NEW CATALINA ISLAND CASINO—2 MILLION DOLLAR PALACE OF PLEASURE.

Postcard, 1930s

Casino building, view from Descanso Bay, 1960s

Avalon Bay, 1998

Mermaid mural execuated in tile

John Gabriel Beckman in front of the
Avalon Theatre Box Office

Casino entrance mural

Foyer, Avalon Theatre

Mural details, Avalon Theatre

Chair detail, Avalon Theatr

Fire curtain, Avalon Theatre

Page Organ, Avalon Theatre

Casino ballroom decorated for the New Year's Eve Ball

Casino balcony

Program, 1935

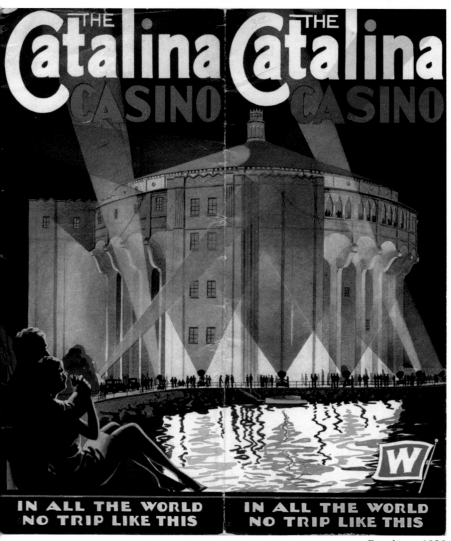

Brochure, 1929

Casino Ballroom dance tickets

The Casino at nigh

C-71   WATER SPORTS AT CATALINA ISLAND, CALIFORNIA

Postcard, 1930

8   The Mezzanine and Other Rooms

In the mezzanine area between the theater and the ballroom are located a cloakroom, ladies' restroom and powder room (to the left of the north ramp), and men's restroom and smoking room (to the right of the south ramp). Beyond the ladies' restroom is the Green Room where performers gather to prepare for their appearances in the ballroom. Beyond the men's restroom is the Band Room where band members had their lockers and preparation area (now used for storage). Both of these rooms have access to the ballroom stage above by way of the fire exits.

Two large alcoves between the restroom complexes contain an exhibit area and the Marine Bar. Originally these areas were waiting rooms where dancers could gather while taking a break. In 1948, when dining and bar facilities were added to the ballroom, these two rooms were redecorated. The current exhibit area was covered with stained, rough-wood paneling to give it a Western décor and named The Corral Room. The Marine Bar also inherited its name and function in 1948, when the Dorothy Shepard marine murals and soda fountain equipment were moved there from the ballroom. In 1986, the Marine Bar was refurbished and decorated with an interpretation of the original murals by local artist Jesse Baily. It can be stocked as a full bar and is used during large ballroom events.

The exhibit area, which was created in 1988, features photo displays of the construction of the building and group pictures of many of the Big Bands that have played in the ballroom. Also on exhibit are original usherette uniforms and equipment from the original radio broadcast booth that sent Big Band music nationwide over the airways. A huge photo mural of the Casino building occupying the center wall of the exhibit area often serves as a backdrop for photographers taking pictures of couples in fancy attire.

Two wide full-length wall mirrors located near the ramps to the ballroom afford opportunities for last minute checks on appearance. The originally bare ramps were covered with wine colored carpeting in the early thirties, but this was removed in 1951. The building's historic Otis freight lelevator makes a stop at mezzanine level on the south ramp. The elevator also stops at ballroom level and is used to provide access for the handicapped during public events.

Below the mezzanine is another level, which would be a little more than halfway up the dome of the theater. Located here, with its entrance door on the south ramp, is the projection room, where a series of projectionists have kept their vigils with the big projectors. Glenn Finney, a member of Local 521 of the Union of Motion Picture Machine Operators, served as the theatre's loyal projectionist from 1987 to 2001.

Ford Harris was projectionist from 1966 to 1986. He trained under M. B. (Nick) Nichols, who was projectionist from 1952 to 1972. Prior to that a series of men filled the position, including Fred Gerehan, Lester Bargaster, Max Miller, Vernon Martz, Glenn Bast, and "Robbie" Robinson. The original projectionist was Dwight Moore. L. M. (Tommy) Thomas started as an assistant projectionist in 1932 and worked up to manager. After Western Amusement Company obtained the lease, he served occasionally as relief projectionist until 1966.

The original Casino manager had an office on the north side of the projection room, with a window into the theater from which he could view the house. Being a man of lavish tastes, he furnished it quite elegantly, even to equipping it with a bar during Prohibition—a fact that may have contributed to his short tenure with the establishment.

Across the vestibule from that famous office, with windows looking out on Descanso Bay, are two approximately 25 x 50 ft. rooms that have had a varied history. The Mormon and Presbyterian Church congregations as well as the Eastern Star and other community groups have held services, meetings, and lectures in them. For several years after World War II, one was also used as a dance studio. In 1978, Catalina Productions Co. leased it for a recording studio. In a small room at the north end of this complex was originally located the control equipment for the public address system that piped sound from the theater and ballroom throughout the building and over the bay.

In 1983, these spaces were consolidated to make an exercise gymnasium. Island Body and Soul Fitness Center provides a compact but complete workout facility. The public entrance to the fitness center is from the ground floor of the building on the ocean side (halfway around the building from the theater entrance) by way of a fire exit.

The corresponding area at this level on the south side of the projection room is used for storage by the Santa Catalina Island Company and the Catalina Island Museum. Below this level are located two film laboratories (entered from the theater lobby) originally set up to process movie footage of the incoming steamer, featuring interviews and other promotional items, to show each night in the theater. Now without equipment, the rooms are used for storage. On the opposite side of the theater lobby at this level are located dressing rooms, two for stars and one for the chorus.

At the top of the south ramp is the apartment of the Director of Casino Operations, entered from a door at the ballroom level next to the kitchen. On the other side of the kitchen, a door leads to a series of rooms at the top of the north ramp which have been living, storage, dressing room, and office spaces over the years. They now comprise the apartment and office for the Ballroom Event Manager for the Casino and Descanso Beach, employed by Catalina Island Resort Services, lessee of the ballroom.

Off the ballroom stage to the left is a radio control room. Here the U.S. Coast Guard installed a radio beacon in 1960. It transmitted the letters "AV" in Morse code at a frequency of 312 kc as a navigation aid for yachtsmen until 1994 when it was dismantled, having been rendered obsolete by modern communications satellite technology. Offstage to the right, stairways lead to spotlight rooms (in one of which CBS set up its first control room for radio broadcasts) then to the attic.

The Ground Floor

The entrance to the Casino is built on a rise that slopes down to a ground floor below the theater auditorium. Four ramps (for emergencies) exit from the theater to the ground level. Around the base of the building, sandwiched between the exit ramps, are numerous rooms with varying histories of occupation.

A Catalina Pottery shop was originally located on the ground floor in the rooms on the north side of the Casino towards Descanso Bay. During World War II, this area was used as an armory. It was remodeled in 1946 to house a boiler for heating the building. After the boiler wore out in the early 1980s, the space was turned into a workshop for the maintenance crew.

Originally, the Santa Catalina Island Company housed its transportation department on the south side facing the freight pier (now the gas dock for boats). Johnny Windle's men dispatched vehicles and supplies from this area. The accounting department, transferred from Wilmington, joined them in 1933. Western Air Express also had space there until 1931.

During World War II, the U.S. Maritime Service used the area as a machine shop. It became a commissary for the new Casino Terrace Restaurant in 1948 and was used as a storage room after that, for a time housing stagecoaches used for parades and special tours. The double doors in the window arches had to be removed to get the coaches in and out and "have never worked the same since."

In 1953, the Catalina Island Museum Society leased the first two rooms on the south side, adding a third room in 1955 and another in 1958. Just beyond, the Catalina Art Association has maintained a small gallery since 1965. This room housed an elaborate miniature railroad from 1951 to 1957. It was constructed by Fire Chief John Hay and KBIG announcer Carl Bailey, both railroad buffs, who gladly gave free demonstrations of their toy to the public.

Subordinate rooms tucked around the great inverted domes of the theater and ballroom on various levels create a marvelous maze with twisting corridors and sudden stairwells. There is probably a square room somewhere in the maze, but most have walls of varying dimensions set at unique angles. This constitutes a source of endless delight and consternation to the people using them.

9   The Ballroom

Cantilever construction makes it possible for the vast expanse of the Casino ballroom to be unbroken by supporting pillars, yet the domed umbrella ceiling and circular space impart a feeling of intimacy that belies the size. The intimate, romantic mood is further enhanced by lighting and decorative detail.

SCI Co, Collection

Repainting the ceiling in 1970

The ceiling shell expands in 32 flutes from a large central chandelier comprised of a circular grille below which hangs a revolving, mirrored cone and four light fixtures. The 38 ft. grille, which conceals the ventilation system, is a sunburst design in pastel shades of peacock blue, apricot, and silver. The ceiling is a warm lavender-gray. The decor and color scheme, as conceived by Gabriel Beckman, was executed by N. A. Walburg of Avalon and his assistants. During a major $600,000 renovation in 1990, under the coordination of Lescht & Associates, Inc. of Chicago, great care was taken to match the original colors when repainting the ceiling.

Hidden colored lights produce pastel shades on the ground-glass plates of the light fixtures. The facets of the central revolving cone reflect and scatter indirect colored lighting from the cove around the grille and from hidden spotlights opposite the bandstand. Additional concealed lighting plays along the fluting of the ceiling. Color patterns and dimness can be controlled from a switchboard behind the bandstand so that the play of colored lights reflects the mood of the music.

CIM Collection

Chandelier detail

The wall, divided into panels corresponding to the flutes of the ceiling,

75

Medallion detail, S.S. Avalon

is broken by 16 glass double-doors leading to the balcony. Originally, the wall panels were royal blue, with apricot pilasters and silver swags. In 1934, when additional acoustical material was added, the royal blue panels were repainted in softer rose tones and have been touched up occasionally since. The terms mauve and peach might best describe the current colors.

The cornice, done in apricot with dentils of silver leaf, and the octagonal modeled-figure plaques that circle the ballroom above door height remain as originally designed. During the 1990 renovation, because of the deteriorated condition of the silver leaf, the modeled-figure plaques were repainted with a special paint containing silver. At that time, the plaque backgrounds, which were alternately red and blue, were repainted and are now all blue. Originally, the doors to the balcony were hung with mauve and gold curtains. These were replaced with prints highlighted with turquoise and rust, which were removed in 1988.

Eva Matysek restoring the medallions

Dancing is delightfully smooth on the circular dance floor laid in strips of maple, white oak, and rosewood in a 16-sided pattern converging toward a central circle. The floor rests on a layer of felt and acoustical paper over a subfloor of polished pine floating above the support beams on strips of cork. It has been well maintained over the years and is in excellent condition.

Originally, three tiers of folding seats behind a balustrade around the perimeter of the dance floor formed a loge, seating about 450 persons. This

CIM Collection

Loge seating in the
ballroom, 1929-1947

area was remodeled in 1947, the seats being replaced with tables and chairs. In addition, a 13-ft. terrace was built around the edge of the floor to hold more tables, thus reducing the dance area from 15,000 to about 10,000 square feet. This new terrace gave rise to the name Casino Terrace Room.

The orchestra shell was originally a half-dome covered with silver leaf that reflected lights from around its edge. Its hard surface caused acoustical problems so it was removed in 1934 and curtains hung at the back and above the front of the stage, which was also enlarged at the time to accommodate the bigger bands. The stage was removed in 1947 and replaced by partially movable, sectioned platforming, with a curved canopy above it. Now, the movable front section also serves as storage for plywood sheets used to protect the dance floor during concerts when rows of European style seating cover the entire area.

Although the acoustics in the new theater were ideal from the beginning, the situation in the ballroom was another matter. Speakers had been placed around the room, concealed behind the octagonal wall plaques. Dancers moving around the floor would hear music from different speakers, thus confusing their beat. Also, when the dance floor was full, reverberations developed that hadn't previously been apparent. The speakers were removed and acoustical engineers installed additional paneling within a month of the opening, improving the acoustics considerably. Further improvements were made in 1934 when radio broadcasts from the ballroom began, including repaneling the last level of the ramps with sound-absorbing material above the wainscot.

During the major remodeling in 1947, the lobby between the two ramps at the entrance to the ballroom was converted into a large kitchen. Five large murals over the lobby entrance depicting the "Dance of Pan" were eliminated in the process and replaced with octagonal plaques. The ramps descending from the terrace to the dance floor were also covered with steps. During the 1990 renovation, mahogany balustrades were added to the stair/ramps and the ballroom was furnished with new tables and chairs. For Jazz Trax and other music festivals, seating capacity is now 1,400 people; for dinner dances such as New Year's Eve, 1,000 people. The kitchen and bars were also refurbished and received new equipment.

The original 1929 lobby had a beamed ceiling, patio tile floor, futuristic decor executed in apricot, turquoise blue, and silver, and boasted a 44 ft. refreshment fountain made of Catalina tile. It was lighted by hanging, box-design fixtures of changeable color and brightness. Girls in costumes matching the decor served refreshing concoctions.

Original Catalina tile soda fountain, 1929, now a kitchen

The Marine Bar in the ballroom, 1935

In 1935, a 100 ft. soft drink fountain replaced the Catalina tile fountain. The lobby was redecorated with murals depicting stylized marine life designed by artist Dorothy Shepard (wife of Philip K. Wrigley's chief advertising artist, Otis Shepard, who gave Crescent Avenue its Early California look). It was dubbed the

78

Marine Bar. The standing bar, equipped with a nickel rail, was done in blue and white with nickel trim. Above the bar, portholes blinked and light reflected from blue mirrors behind the fountain manned by lads in nautical caps and white uniforms.

Since 1948, when the Casino Terrace Room briefly served dinners and began serving alcoholic beverages, a service bar for drinks has been located on either side of the entrance to the kitchen. Now when catering for large parties, long buffet tables are set up along the tiers below the service bars.

The 14 ft. balcony encircling the ballroom has not changed substantially, although weathering has required some repainting and the Catalina patio tile floors with figure insets have become worn by seven decades of use. Around the 18 ft. high ceiling are 25 panels, originally laid in silver leaf, but redone in silver paint during the 1990 renovation. The cornices are in ebony decorated with ivory futuristic figures and trimmed with peacock blues and vermilion, touched up most recently during the 1990 renovation. Beams and lintels adorn the concrete walls between the rose-trimmed door arches.

The balcony affords magnificent views from Descanso Beach to Avalon Bay. On a clear day visitors can see the mainland. Sometimes in the winter Mt. Baldy and Saddleback loom snowcapped in the distance.

Dancing at the Casino

Millions of visitors to Catalina over the years cherish memories of dancing at the Casino, a tribute to William

CIM Collection

A Sunday matinee dance, 1929

Dancing to the music of Curt Houck, 1932

Wrigley Jr., who encouraged entertainment the whole family could enjoy. To this end, the new Casino was operated with the utmost propriety. Dress codes were strictly enforced. Gentlemen were admitted to the ballroom only if wearing coats and ties; ladies, of course, wore suitable dresses—no trousers. Naturally, tales survive of neckties tossed over the balcony to fellow yachtsmen, of shoes hidden then lost by those who could only "really" dance in their bare feet, and, inevitably, of hip flasks.

Actually, the building was well policed by a special deputation of the local constabulary. The ballroom floor manager circulated among the dancers, assuring that proper distance and decorum were maintained. Alcoholic beverages were not served in the building, even after repeal of Prohibition in 1933, and those "under the influence" by whatever means were escorted away quietly.

Far from spoiling the fun, maintenance of a decorous atmosphere enhanced the reputation of the ballroom. Virginia Renton recalled many an evening spent dancing at the Casino while she was a young Avalon school teacher. Because of its refinement—dancers were considered guests of the Wrigleys—this was the only ballroom in the Long Beach School

Dancing in late 1930's

Menu from the Marine Bar

District considered suitable for teachers to attend. The original floor manager, Larry Paper, elegant in his tuxedo, also acted as a gracious host. He was a splendid dancer and a turn with him was the highlight of many a girl's evening. Later floor managers vied to maintain the tradition he established.

It was perfectly acceptable for singles as well as couples to go to the dance. The ballroom was a place for mixing and meeting; it was quite proper to dance with strangers. Dancers could rest in the loge between sets or refresh themselves at the soda fountain with fancy sundaes—"Wrigley Welcome," "Casino Surprise," or "Avalon Temptation"—as well as ades, phosphates, and sodas. Or they could stroll along the balcony, enjoying the cool breeze and the view of the yachts in the beautiful moonlit bay.

The atmosphere was gay and friendly and very romantic. Colored lights played over the dancers in rhythm with the sweet sounds of the bands. Bandleaders talked to their audiences, announcing songs, introducing guests, conducting sing-alongs. Often couples gathered around the bandstand to listen to the vocalists or specialty numbers. Over the years the bandleaders developed elaborate entertainment features with skits, costumes, games, and quizzes, including audience participation, to amuse a vast radio audience as well as the ballroom guests. Catalina with its beautiful Casino was a honeymoon paradise.

CIM Collection

U.S. Maritime Service Christmas dance, World War II

After World War II, an attempt was made to return to prewar dress standards. For a time, the necktie rental business (50¢ an evening) flourished. But styles and habits changed, and by 1949, men were allowed in the ballroom wearing jackets (no sweaters) but no ties, although women were still not admitted in slacks. Casual dress won the day a year later. After that a mixture of dress styles was seen on the dance floor.

The addition of tables and cocktails after the war gave the ballroom more of a nightclub atmosphere, albeit respectable. Although entertainment and musical tastes continued to change rapidly, with vocalists, singing groups, and rock stars replacing Big Band leaders as musical celebrities, some Big Bands survived. They continued to draw good crowds at the ballroom into the 1960's. On big weekends, the smaller dance floor would often be crowded with over 2,000 dancers.

Since 1965, there has been no nightly public dancing for adults in the ballroom, although Big Bands are still booked for one-night stands for holidays and benefits. Visitors to the Island have, however, been able to enjoy an increasing number of weekend music festivals. Jazz Trax, perhaps the premier smooth jazz festival in the country, has been held each October since 1987 and now runs three weekends.

Dancing in the Casino Terrace Room, 1948

Although there is less smooth dancing, the ballroom is not often dark. Community groups use it frequently and it is being increasingly booked for corporate parties, with mainland organizations such as Voit, Centex Homes, and Toyota, returning year after year. The setting has become a favorite for weddings, quinceneros (major parties within the Latino culture celebrating a girl's fifteenth birthday), and Christmas parties. Some elaborate weddings have cost as much as $250,000.

In 1994, James Cameron, the producer and writer of the hit movie *Titanic*, rented the ballroom on Valentine's Day to propose to actress Linda

Hamilton. Naturally, he brought in set decorators, caterers, and musicians to help orchestrate a romantic dinner for two on a grand scale.

Dress styles have become increasingly casual in recent years and many attend concerts and rock or country dances in the ballroom in whatever they happen to have on at the moment, their apparel in sharp contrast to their elegant surroundings. There are still occasions, however, when couples will arrive at the Casino in black tie and ball gown to attend such galas as the Tuna Club Centennial, the annual Santa Catalina Island Conservancy Ball, or the building's longest standing tradition, the New Year's Eve Dance. (The millennium New Year's Eve event was sold out two years in advance.)

For some with long memories, the romance of the ballroom may have dimmed with the demise of nightly dancing, but for thousands new to the scene, the "pleasure chest" still yields many bright jewels of delight.

CIM Collection

Ballroom terrace

10 The Big Bands

The list of the Big Bands that have played at the Catalina Casino is lengthy and impressive. New names are still being added. However, to Maurice Menge and his El Patio-Catalina Orchestra goes the honor of having officially opened the Casino Ballroom on May 29, 1929. This band from the famous El Patio Ballroom in Los Angeles had pleased a capacity crowd including Mr. and Mrs. Wrigley Jr. during a January audition at Avalon's Riviera Theatre.

On the Saturday before the official opening, Islanders had been treated to a special preview of the magnificent building that had so rapidly taken shape before their fascinated eyes. About 2,500 Islanders and visitors toured the building and spent a delightful evening dancing to the music of Frank Hobbs and the Hotel St. Catherine Orchestra. Many still recall proudly that they were the very first to dance in Mr. Wrigley's new Casino.

Opening ceremonies for the rest of the world the next week were lavish, and the new ballroom was an instant success. By mid-June the dance floor was so crowded one Saturday night that the old Pavilion dance hall near the Pleasure Pier was opened and provided with an orchestra to handle the overflow. In July an appeal appeared in the local newspaper urging Islanders to let visitors use the new Casino during the crush of the season. The average Saturday crowd during August was estimated at 5,480 persons; weeknight crowds averaged 3,000 persons. Even the New Year's Eve Masque Ball attracted 2,000 revelers.

The El Patio-Catalina Orchestra played for free dancing nightly through the summer. They also gave afternoon concerts in the open air Greek Amphitheatre across town and continued the longtime tradition of serenading the afternoon steamer as it left Avalon Bay. Former band members Jack Baptiste, Maury Paul, and Lank Menge (brother of the orchestra's director, Maurice) recalled that with so much activity their white suits (worn with orange neckties and handkerchiefs and two-toned shoes) rapidly became soiled. Sent to the mainland for cleaning, they were washed by mistake and shrank. Latecomers to work the next day ended up with short cuffs and visible socks.

Prohibition was in force and some members of the band were found to have "leaky suitcases" or pints stashed in their quarters—the cabins near the ballpark that housed the Chicago Cubs during spring training. Local tradition has it that for this reason the group did not continue beyond the height of the season. The three former band members recalled closing night when they abandoned their season's restrained repertoire of waltzes and fox trots and jazzed it up—playing *Twelfth Street Rag* and similar tunes. The crowd, containing many Islanders, loved it and complained that the band hadn't played that way before. The same sort of story is told about the Benny Goodman Band, which "cut loose" on the last engagement of a lukewarm tour in 1935 and turned the crowd wild—starting the rage for swing.

The outdoor concerts played by the El Patio-Catalina Orchestra were also quite popular throughout the summer. Essentially a dance band, they had added a string section and the necessary instrumentation for a small concert orchestra and played concert arrangements of popular tunes and music from current musical shows, along with light classical selections. Maury Paul recalled that occasionally they got overly ambitious, once trying Grieg's *Peer Gynt Suite.* All went well until the last movement, which the conductor took at a breakneck pace. "We finished raggedly but almost together about two measures ahead of the poor tuba player who bravely soloed to the end. The audience applauded loyally, probably thinking this was our special touch."[9] When Menge finished his engagement on September 14, the orchestra went on to the Roosevelt Hotel where they were heard by representatives of 20th Century Fox Studios and were hired to do its first "all star" musical.

At the Casino, Frank Hobbs augmented the Hotel St. Catherine Orchestra by three members and played for nightly dancing during the winter. The following May, Hobbs formed the Catalina Concert Orchestra, with Benito Kaitz as director, and provided music for nightly dancing at the Casino Ballroom for the next two years. The orchestra also played for dinner dancing at Hotel St. Catherine, gave concerts, and serenaded the steamer. Favorite parting songs were *Avalon, Aloha,* and a popular new tune, *Catalina, Lovely Isle of the Sea,* written by Elizabeth (Mrs. D. M.) Renton and by George Crozier, who had been an arranger with the

Capolungo Catalina Symphonette in 1928. (Al, Paul, and Ralph Capolungo, a father and two sons, had orchestras that played on the steamers and in Avalon during the late 1920's and 1930's.)

Curt Houck and his orchestra opened at the Casino on June 27, 1932. Houck was the son of a Los Angeles advertising man acquainted with the Wrigleys. When he was playing at Catalina, his young orchestra and the Casino were advertised on bus signs in the Southland. When he went on tour, his "Catalina Casino" music was advertised on bus signs all around the country, for the J. C. Houck Motor Coach Company handled all bus advertising in the United States.

Houck and his orchestra played for the 1932 and 1933 summer seasons. He caught the fancy of the collegiate set and soon drew large crowds. D. M. Renton wrote to J. C. Houck in 1932 that Curt had played to 16,400 people in two

Curt Houck's band advertisement rides the bus

days (July 3-4) and praised his music, saying, "it does not have the blare that a great many bands do, and goes well with the acoustics of the Casino."[10]

Vocalists in the Houck band with megaphones

Both years Houck played, Frankie Gould brought his orchestra from the Crystal Ballroom in Long Beach over for a guest appearance and over a thousand followers came with him each time.

Arthur Renton sang with the Houck orchestra during the summers. (Then a student at Pomona College, he later went on to a successful musical career.) His brother Malcolm remembered that the band members wore white Panama suits and that Arthur used a white megaphone covered with sparkles. The kaleidoscope of colored lights from the central chandelier played across the white-costumed band to great effect.

With The Depression at its worst, the great ballroom was too large for the dwindling weeknight crowds. During the winter of 1933, an orchestra formed by Hal Rees, formerly an arranger for Curt Houck, held forth at the cozier Hotel St. Catherine on Monday, Wednesday, and Friday, playing for dancing at the Casino only on Tuesday, Thursday, and Saturday.

Efforts to make Catalina into a year round resort met with little success in face of the economic situation, and the next year the Santa Catalina Island Company bowed to the forces of seasonality and closed the ballroom during the winter. However, Philip K. Wrigley established the very successful pattern of engaging a series of bands each summer and having their music broadcast nationwide over the radio.

Jan Garber Orchestra, 1937

Three well-known bands played six-week engagements at the ballroom in 1934. Irving Aaronson and his Commanders opened on May 15, Jan Garber on July 2, and Hal Grayson, "the Melody Master," on August 27. These bands had all been heard over the radio and were gaining nationwide reputations. This was Garber's first appearance on the West Coast, and he quickly proved a great favorite at the Casino, playing to crowds of 3 to 5,000 persons nightly. He returned four years in a row, and it soon became a moot point whether he or the Casino benefited more from the happy association. There was now an admission charge of 25¢ for dancing on week nights and 40¢ on weekends. In 1935, a combination ticket for 50¢ gave access to both the theater and ballroom. For Sunday matinee dancing, 25¢ was charged.

Garber was gaining fame, but Ben Bernie was touted as having the highest paid band in the nation when he opened at the Casino on May 25, 1935. The era of the Big Bands had begun. Bandleaders became celebrities on a par with movie stars, whom they often married, and their names were the staples of gossip columns. Bands toured the world and became international hits. Ben Bernie, "the Ole Maestro," charmed millions with his outrageous quips and running feud with Walter Winchell.

Jan Garber, now truly the "Idol of the Air Lanes," followed Bernie at the Casino on July 2. Handsome Buddy Rogers arrived on August 20 with his California Cavaliers to finish the season. He carried on his courtship of Mary Pickford in Catalina waters aboard Mr. Wrigley's yacht *Quest.*

Little Jack Little, that "Cheerful Little Earful," opened the Casino on May 23, 1936. He was followed on July 2 by Jan Garber, who had become a Catalina institution. Garber played until mid-September, setting new records for attendance.

Dick Jurgens, "the Crown Prince of Rhythm," opened the Casino on May 22, 1937, and soon proved popular. Jan Garber returned on July 1 for an eight-week engagement. Herbie Kay made his first appearance in the Southland with a two-week engagement in September to end the season. His wife, the glamorous actress Dorothy Lamour, thrilled audiences by appearing as his guest.

Roger Pryor opened the 1938 season on May 21 and was followed on June 18 by Dick Jurgens, who now rivaled Garber as a Catalina favorite. Ted Weems, the jitterbug idol, arrived on August 6 to finish the season. His singing sextet included that handsome young Italian, Perry Como.

Dick Jurgens Orchestra, 1939

The Casino celebrated its 10th anniversary in 1939. Kay Kyser opened the ballroom on May 20, his first appearance on the Pacific Coast since he had gained fame. Ted Weems followed on June 18; then Freddy Martin arrived on August 6 to play until mid-September.

Kay Kyser returned in 1940 to open the Casino on May 18, playing to some 6,200 people on opening night. He was followed by Benny Goodman,

Kay Kyser Orchestra, 1939

"the King of Swing," on June 16. Dick Jurgens arrived on July 14, and Bob Crosby and the Bob Cats followed on August 11 for a six week engagement.

Freddy Martin Orchestra, 1939

Ray Noble chased away thoughts of war with his sweet sounds as he opened the Casino on May 17, 1941. Dick Jurgens returned for the fourth time on June 15. Hal Grayson started on July 13—young Rudy Vallee was one of his guest vocalists. Bob Crosby and the Bob Cats returned on August 10 to play the last peacetime engagement in the beautiful Casino Ballroom.

Benny Goodman Orchestra, 1940

The season was spectacular during the "golden age" of the Big Bands, but there were also successful balls at other times of the year. The President's Birthday Ball, for Franklin D. Roosevelt, a benefit for the fight against infantile paralysis, was held in the spring of 1935 and continued yearly. Music for this and other benefits was usually provided by the Frank Sortino or Capolungo orchestras.

CIM Collection

Kate Smith on the Avalon Pier, 1940's

During World War II, dances were held fairly regularly in the ballroom. (In town, Virginia Renton, along with other local volunteers, organized other activities for the recruits for two years before the USO assumed the responsibility.) Many top entertainers gave benefit performances for the trainees. Alice Faye joined her husband, Lt. Phil Harris, U.S. Maritime Services bandleader, to entertain the boys in 1942. Kay Kyser, Bob Hope, Kate Smith, Bob Burns, Earl Carroll, and Ted Weems were among the many who entertained in 1943.

Kay Kyser returned in 1944, along with Danny Kaye, Dick Powell, and Johnny Mercer, with singer Jo Stafford. Spike Jones and his City Slickers, Dick Haymes with the Gordon Jenkins Orchestra and guest conductor David Rose, and David Forrester's Hollywood Canteen Symphony Orchestra were among the 1945 entertainers to appear before the war ended and the training camps disbanded. Townspeople were sometimes invited to the wartime shows and dances.

The 1946 season at Catalina was one of the busiest ever, a rush of postwar relief. Jimmy Grier, "the Musical Host of the Coast," opened the Casino on May 29 for a six-week engagement. Leighton Noble followed on July 20, playing "Noble Music." Carlos Molina offered a week of Latin American rhythms and ended the season on September 14. Admission to the dancing was 90¢ plus tax.

Leighton Noble returned to open the Casino on May 30, 1947, and played through July. Then a "house" group was formed—under the leadership of Caesar Petrillo. In September, the Miss Catalina swimsuit company chartered the SS *Avalon* to bring the press and wholesale buyers to a private showing of their 1948 swimsuit line, featuring 80 models. In 1948, Don Ricardo, who had become popular with Catalina visitors when his orchestra played for crossings on the steamer, led his Catalina Terrace Orchestra. He played in a remodeled ballroom with a reduced dance area.

Don Ricardo Orchestra, 1948

The Island was attracting increasing crowds at Easter, so in 1949 the Chuck Cabot Orchestra was engaged to provide music for a week of nightly dancing. The Casino Terrace Room opened again for the season on May 27 with the return of that old island favorite, Jan Garber, who began a ten-week engagement with an opening crowd of 3,400 persons. Leighton Noble, returning for the third time, ended the season with a two - week engagement. Admission was now $1.20, including tax.

Milt Herth Trio, 1950

Chuck Cabot played at the Casino again for Easter Week of 1950, then the season started on May 27 with a double billing. The Milt Herth Trio, with Milt at the electric organ, on an especially built side stage, alternated each evening with Dick Cavanaugh's newly formed Dixieland group, The Curbstone Cops. This was the first time two orchestras were featured regularly for a whole season. Dancing was free and attracted large crowds—2,000 the first night, and a record night for the season of 4,835 persons.

Curbstone Cops, 1950

In 1951, a pattern of one-night stands and short engagements was tried. The Casino opened for Memorial Day weekend with Ina Ray Hutton and her orchestra. Dances on Saturday nights in June featured different bands—Lorraine Cugat, The Firehouse Five Plus Two, and Garwood Van with singer Dick Haymes. Woody Herman played nightly the last week in June, followed by Stan Kenton, Jimmy Dorsey, Matty Malneck, Tony Pastor, and Ray Whitaker, ending on Labor Day.

Lorraine Cugat Orchestra, 1951

The Casino Ballroom was "dark" in 1952, a low point in its illustrious career as a pleasure palace. Yet even then several benefit dances were sponsored by local organizations such as the Lions Club, Catholic Church, and Chamber of Commerce. Local mainland orchestras such as those of Bob Mohr, Burrell Ubbens, and Ray Broggie were featured. Don Ricardo and his orchestra played for the Motorcycle Racers Ball in early May.

During the late 1940's and 1950's, the St. Patrick's Day and March of Dimes Balls were particularly popular off-season events. The Flying Fish

Festival, Motorcycle Races, and Buccaneer Days were also occasions for dances. Orchestras led by Bob Mohr, Kay Riggs, Don Ricardo, and Sterling Young, among others, played at the Casino for these dances. Groups such as the "Smooth Dancers" and the "Square Dancers" also enjoyed the ballroom regularly.

There was a series of Saturday night dances from Easter through July Fourth in 1953, then Johnny David and his Catalinians played for dancing Thursday, Friday, and Saturday nights through Labor Day. This pattern was repeated in 1954, with Johnny David again playing, this time from Memorial Day through Labor Day. Henry Busse and the King Sisters also put in an appearance that year. Charlie Barnett and his orchestra played the season of 1956; Ray Noval, the season of 1957; and Claude Gordon, the season of 1958. Crowds on non-holidays averaged from 5 to 800 persons—the high school set dancing on Thursday nights when admission was 60¢; the older set on Friday and Saturday nights when admission was $1.00.

Russ Morgan Orchestra, 1961

Dancing was increased to five nights a week from July through Labor Day in 1959. Jerry Grey and his Band of Today were featured, playing nightly except Sunday and Monday. As usual, various organizations sponsored occasional Saturday night dances before and after the season. Don Ricardo played for the Catalina Art Association "Moon and Sixpence" Ball in late October.

CIM Collection

Fletcher Henderson Orchestra, 1961

In 1960, Terry Gibbs and his sixteen-piece orchestra played four nights a week, starting Memorial Day, until the Eddy Grady orchestra took over in mid-July and played until mid-September. Russ Morgan returned for the 1961 season, starting Memorial Day, with a bevy of guest stars including Frankie Lane, Tony Martin, Giselle MacKenzie, Gogi Grant, and the Mary Kaye Trio. Fletcher Henderson also played at the Casino that year. Prices were now $1.00 Tuesday to Thursday and Sunday matinee, $1.50 Friday, and $2.00 Saturday. Buffet luncheons and dinners were also served.

In 1962, the Eddy Howard orchestra played nightly, except Sunday and Monday, from mid-June until the Johnny Catron orchestra took over in August. Russ Morgan played for the summer of 1963 and returned for the Catalina Art Festival costume ball later in the fall.

Eddie Allen and his orchestra played Tuesday through Saturday from July Fourth through Labor Day in 1964. Ray Noval played Fridays and Saturdays the same months in 1965, and provided music Tuesdays through Thursdays in the Mirror Room of the Hotel St. Catherine. These bands also gave afternoon concerts and serenaded the departing steamer in the afternoon.

Two outstanding musical events occurred in the Casino Ballroom in these years that offered a decided change of musical pace. The Los Angeles Philharmonic Orchestra, with Franz Waxman, conductor, and Malcolm Frazer, guest piano soloist, gave performances in the ballroom in October of 1960. The musicians were arranged in the center of the dance floor. The acoustics were perfect for symphonic performance and delighted the conductor and musicians as well as the audience. A performance of Shakespeare's *A Midsummer Night's Dream,* starring Jack Carson and June Lockhart, was also part of the program. In September, 1964, the Long Beach Symphony Orchestra also gave a concert in the ballroom with great success.

From 1966 through 1974 there was no regularly scheduled public dancing in the Casino for adults. Various convention groups renting the ballroom held private dances, and the Chamber of Commerce sponsored New Year's Eve dances and an occasional Memorial Day, July Fourth, or Labor Day dance. A highlight was the appearance of Count Basie on July 4-5, 1971. An annual Dixieland Jazz Festival was started in 1972. During an International Fiesta each spring, the ballroom was filled with colorful performing folk dance groups.

CIM Collection

Count Basie Orchestra, 1971

Newt Perry, who then owned the Glenmore Hotel in Avalon, appeared with his orchestra for Labor Day in 1973 and 1974. During this decade, however, the younger set enjoyed the Casino Ballroom regularly at rock and roll "teen" dances sponsored by the City of Avalon. Local mainland bands with imaginative names provided amplified sounds quite different from those of the Big Bands.

Then, in 1975, Chamber of Commerce posters announced: "The Big Bands are Back!" The Johnny Catron, Les Brown, Freddy Martin, and Jimmy Dorsey (directed by Lee Castle) orchestras were booked for one-night stands at the Casino and played to increasing crowds as the word spread. Tickets sold for $6.50. The Big Band sound still had appeal, and ballroom dancing was experiencing a revival around the country. To the amusement of their elders, college students were enrolling in classes to learn the steps to which their parents had fallen in love.

In 1976, the list of Big Bands appearing at the Casino grew longer: Freddy Martin, Les Brown, Harry James, Glenn Miller (directed by Jimmy Henderson), and Woody Herman. Chamber of Commerce manager Lita Utal was encouraged as attendance increased. Ticket sales had to be limited to avoid overcrowding, even though the price had increased to $7.50. Youth dances, benefits, and private conventions also continued in the historic ballroom.

The Chamber of Commerce sponsored more dances in 1977, featuring Bob Crosby and the Bob Cats, and the Jimmy Dorsey (directed by Lee Castle), Glenn Miller (directed by Jimmy Henderson), Freddy Martin, Les Brown, and Harry James orchestras. The annual Dixieland Jazz Jamboree packed the ballroom for July 30-31. Tracy Wells and "That Big Band" filled the Casino for a New Year's Eve gala.

Responding to the revival, the Chamber sponsored ten dances in 1978, featuring the Alvino Rey, Russ Morgan (directed by Jack Morgan), Nelson Riddle, Glenn Miller (directed by Jimmy Henderson), Jimmy Dorsey (directed by Lee Castle), and Freddy Martin orchestras, and four appearances by Tracy Wells, who was becoming a favorite with Avalon

Alvino Rey Orchestra, 1978

98

visitors. As in the two previous years, the last dance in September, featuring the Freddy Martin Orchestra, was a sellout benefit for Avalon Municipal Hospital.

In addition to the Big Bands there was another Dixieland Jazz Jamboree and a Country Western Jamboree, featuring Cliffie Stone and the Sons of the Pioneers. To increase the variety of sounds flowing down the shell of the venerable ballroom, Disco Fantasy (dancing to recorded music orchestrated by a disc jockey) came to the Casino in 1978. Flashing lights were added and the young of all ages were invited to dance to disco sounds several evenings a week during August and September.

For the 50th anniversary year of the Casino, the Chamber manager booked twelve more dance events: The King Zulu Paraders (who play for the New Orleans Mardi Gras), a Country Western dance in conjunction with the Chili Cook-Off, Bob Crosby and the Bob Cats, the Alvino Rey and Jimmy Dorsey (directed by Lee Castle) orchestras, A Little Country/A Little Rock & Roll, the Freddy Martin and Bill Tole orchestras, and four appearances by the Tracy Wells Big Band, the last being the traditional New Year's Eve gala. The Dixieland Jazz Jamboree marked its 8th year and Disco Fantasy continued. The Casino Ballroom offered sounds for the old to remember—or the young to discover—along with new rhythms for the "now generation" as it marked its Golden Anniversary.

In the following decade, interest in the Big Band sound began to wane again and it was harder to fill the Casino ballroom with dancing couples. The Freddy Martin Orchestra played for the Avalon Hospital Benefit each September through 1983. Alvino Rey did the honors in 1984; Lou Catalano & The Sound Investment Band from 1985 through 1987; and Bill Davies & his Orchestra in 1988, the last year the event was held.

Tracy Wells and That Big Band, an Avalon favorite, played for the Halloween Costume Ball from 1980 through 1983, then a series of less well-known groups provided the music for this traditional event. Big Band sounds seem to go with Valentine's Day and that special occasion has been celebrated most years with a dance. Tracy Wells, Alvino Rey, Bob Crosby and the Bob Cats, and The Mar Dels have all played for this dance.

Tracy Wells and That Big Band, popular in the 1980's

Big Bands that played on various other occasions during 1980 include the Jimmy Dorsey (under Lee Castle), Tracy Wells, and Bill Tole Orchestras, Bob Crosby and the Bob Cats, and the Ed Leach Big Swing Band for New Year's Eve. In 1981, the Jimmy Dorsey (under Lee Castle) and Bill Tole Orchestras appeared again along with Fred Nied & The Yachtsmen, the Alvino Rey and Joe Diamond Orchestras, and Tino Isgro & All the King's Saxes. Alvino Rey and His Orchestra played again for New Year's Eve.

New bands in 1982 included Claude Gordon, His Trumpet and His Orchestra and the Bill Davies and Pat Longo Orchestras. Alvino Rey and Tino Isgro returned. The Bill Davies Orchestra returned in 1983, and Alvino Rey & His Orchestra played for New Year's Eve that year. The Harry James Orchestra played twice in 1984. Lee Castle with the Jimmy Dorsey Orchestra was back, and the Newport Society Band made its first appearance. Alvino Rey & His Orchestra played for New Year's Eve in 1985. The Société Big Band helped ring in the new year in 1986; the Gene Krupa Orchestra, in 1987.

SCI Co. Collection

Bill Davies Orchestra, 1990's

In 1988, Les Elgart & His Orchestra, the Artie Shaw Orchestra, the Vaughn Monroe Orchestra, and the Joe Diamond Band provided the Big Band sounds for the Casino Ballroom. The Modernaires offered Music in the Miller Mood for New Year's Eve. In 1989, for the Casino's 60th anniversary year, The Rhythm Kings played for New Year's Eve. They returned to ring in the new year again in 1990 and 1991. The Bill Davies Orchestra played for an Afternoon Tea Dance in 1991. Horace Heidt Jr. & His Orchestra played for an Afternoon Tea Dance in 1992 and Art Deco & his Orchestra played for New Year's Eve.

Afternoon Tea Dances continued in vogue in 1993, with Horace Heidt Jr. & his Orchestra and Jay Ware & The Peninsulas doing the honors. Art Deco & His Society Orchestra played for New Year's Eve. In 1994, The Kicks played for an Afternoon Tea Dance. That year not just the ballroom but venues all over Avalon were alive with the Big Band sound when the Pasadena Ballroom Dance Association held a three-day swing camp on the Island. The Bill Elliott Swing Orchestra held forth in the ballroom as the younger generation learned to swing. (The increasingly popular swing camp has become an annual event and the Bill Elliott Orchestra has returned every year.) Later that year, the Memo Bernabei Orchestra played for the Ballroom Dancers group. (Bernabei used to play with the popular Jan Garber.) Art Deco & His Orchestra played for New Year's Eve.

In 1995, the Armand Blais Orchestra played for a series of Afternoon Tea Dances, and Les Brown and His Band of Renown played for the first annual Santa Catalina Island Conservancy Ball. The first ball was a great success, filling the ballroom with gentlemen in black tie and ladies in beautiful gowns. Each year since then one of the many yacht clubs that frequent Catalina's beautiful coves has sponsored the ball, each vying to outdo the other in raising funds for the Conservancy. Les Brown and His Band of Renown has returned every year for this gala that rivals the New Year's Eve dance as the event to attend.

Maintaining the ballroom's oldest tradition, the Horace Heidt Orchestra played for New Year's Eve in 1995, followed by The Yachtsmen in 1996, 1997, and 1998. Tickets for the New Year's Eve dance usually go on sale in October and the event is sold out within the month. Tickets were sold out a year in advance for New Year's Eve 1999, when The American Swing Orchestra, A Musical Salute to Benny Goodman, directed by Clem DeRosa, helped bring in the new millennium and celebrate the 70th anniversary year of the Casino ballroom.

Concerts and Festivals

Big Band sounds may emanate from the historic ballroom less frequently these days, but the elegant umbrella shell is far from silent. In 1983, the ballroom had a remarkable year as a concert venue. Amoroso Productions (owners of the local Glenmore Hotel) brought The Righteous Brothers to the Casino for a 20th reunion concert, then booked Merlin Jazz, Three Dog Night, The James Harmon Band, and Jack Mack & the Heart Attack. These well-known names in rock 'n roll, blues, and rhythm & blues drew good crowds.

Television personality and singer John Davidson, then at the height of his career, packed the ballroom that year with a benefit concert he put on for the local Chamber of Commerce. For several years, Davidson had held a summer camp for singers on the campus of the Catalina Island School at Toyon Bay and had become so well-known and liked in Avalon that the City Council made him an honorary mayor. (Davidson has the distinction of having been gored by a Catalina bison, a feat he accomplished during an encounter in the hills which he tried to turn into a photo opportunity. To his credit, the reckless toreador graciously acknowledged that the bison was only acting in self-defense.)

Also appearing in 1983 were John Sebastian (folk singer); The Drifters (rhythm & blues and pop singers); and Dave Mason (pop singer and writer). The variety of entertainment continued in 1984. Pop drummer Mick Fleetwood and his Zoo energized the crowd in August. A "copy" band, The Rolling Clones (which mimics carefully the sounds, gestures, and dress of the superstar performers), was booked twice, and other rock bands had their nights in the spotlight.

Two well-known groups, The Drifters and the Box Tops, appeared together twice in 1985, and the Shirelles, a female Pop group, thrilled the crowd on July Fourth. The Cotton Club Show, which featured The Ink Spots, was a highlight of 1987. The Dixieland Jazz Jamboree continued to draw its devoted fans, as did the Country Western Dance. A bright spot in 1987 was the first Jazz Trax Festival (a weekend of smooth jazz concert performances) brought to the Casino by radio personality Art Good.

Big Jay McNeely, a Jazz & Blues saxophonist popular in the States since the 1950s and a great hit in the Scandinavian countries, packed the Casino twice in 1988, on July Fourth and Labor Day. Veteran performer McNeely is known for leaving the stage and walking through the audience while playing. (He took a liking to the Island and continues to appear either at the Casino or other venues around Avalon.) The Dixieland Jazz Jamboree and Country Western Dance continued as staples that year, and the second annual Jazz Trax Festival made a strong showing.

The year 1988 also marked the debut of the annual Plein Air Art Festival in the Casino ballroom. For two days every November the ballroom floor is ringed with lighted easels displaying freshly painted scenes of Avalon and Santa Catalina Island. Artists, art lovers, and dealers, enjoy dinner accompanied by soft music from a string quartet then set about the business of viewing the paintings. The next day, brunch is served and more paintings are on view. The experience is music to the eyes.

The Plein Air Painters of America was formed by a local artist, Denise Burns, in 1986, along with the Festival, as part of a revival of artistic interest in painting in the open air (en plein air) as opposed to the studio. The roots of plein air painting go back to the Impressionist movement in Europe in the 18th century. The United States and California, in particular, boasted respectable schools of plein air painters in the early years of the 19th century. Many well-known scenes of Catalina were created during that time; then art tastes changed.

Now, the circle has turned again and each year thirty top artists spend a week on the island painting out-of-doors with great concentration. Artists and easels can be found all over Avalon and in quiet scenic places in the hills. Amazingly, the scenes are fresh and new each time the artists display their work in the ballroom. Sales are brisk and the event is usually sold out well in advance. The beautifully renovated ballroom is a perfect venue for this festival.

The Casino celebrated its 60th anniversary in 1989 with The Four Preps in concert for Memorial Day. This group holds a special place in the hearts of Islanders because of their hit recording in the 1960s of *Twenty-six Miles*

The Four Preps at the 60th Anniversary Concert

Across the Sea, a song about Catalina as well known to younger generations as *Avalon* was during the heyday of the Big Bands.

Local musician and promoter Malcolm Jones also booked some top entertainment into the ballroom in 1989, starting with Stephen Stills in concert for July Fourth. The guitarist, singer, and songwriter (of Crosby, Stills, & Nash fame) packed the house. Over the Labor Day weekend, he booked The Turtles (Pop singers) one night and John Mayall (harmonica, guitar) and Spencer Davis (guitar) the next. Old staples included the Dixieland Jazz Jamboree and Country Western Dance.

Keiko Matsui performing at Jazz Traxx, 1989

In its third year, the Jazz Trax Festival, scheduled the first weekend in October, was gaining popularity. Smooth Jazz was coming into its own with the help of top performers like The Rippingtons Band, Acoustic Alchemy, and Keiko Matsui. Producer Art Good had mastered the logistics of staging performances on an island and his widely syndicated radio show had a strong following of smooth jazz aficionados.

The popular Four Preps appeared again on Valentine's Day in 1990, the year the ballroom underwent a major refurbishment. Malcolm Jones booked a sell-out Steppenwolf & John Kay Concert in July of 1991. Television personality John Tesh staged a spectacular light and sound concert in October of 1996 to air on public television during pledge drives. The event took two days to film and locals and mainland visitors packed the ballroom both evenings.

The USC Marching Band began a tradition of participating in the local Fourth of July parade in 1990, and also continue to entertain delighted fans in the ballroom, drill team included, before the evening fireworks are enjoyed from the Casino balcony. The Dixieland Jazz Jamboree attracted devotees every July until 1996, when its indefatigable producer, Hal Rumenapp, died. Richie Havens appeared in concert in 1998, bringing back memories of Woodstock. Willie Chambers was on the same bill. Beatlemania, a show that follows the immortal Beatles through time (complete with costume changes), also made a hit in 1998 and returned again in 1999, along with Sticky Fingers, a Rolling Stones copy group.

Jazz Trax, which has grown to be one of the premier smooth jazz festivals in the nation thanks to the dedicated efforts of Art Good, was expanded to two weekends in October in 1991, and three weekends in 1999. During the festival, entertainers perform not just in the ballroom, but in the mezzanine bar and Avalon Theatre as well. Smooth jazz lovers from around the country often plan their vacations to include the festival. The event also attracts people in the

The Rippingtons at Jazz Traxx

radio and record business, so a number of up and coming performers have gotten their big break by being heard at Catalina Jazz Trax.

The long list of outstanding smooth jazz performers includes such greats as Grover Washington, Jr. (saxophone), Acoustic Alchemy (a London group of two guitarists and a band), Joe Sample (keyboardist), Hiroshima (a Japanese group), Peter White (guitar), Keiko Matsui (Japanese keyboardist), Jesse Cook (Canadian French classical guitarist), Bob James (piano), Willie & Lobo (guitar & violin), Boney James (saxophone), Marc Antoine (French classical guitar), and David Sanborn (saxophone).

The success of the music festival format led to the inauguration of the Fender Catalina Island Blues Festival in 1997, with such Blues greats as Jimmy Vaughn, Jim Belushi & the Sacred Hearts, and the Alexander Band.

CIM Collection

Blues Festival Poster

In 1998, the annual May event featured, among others, Jonny Lang, Buddy Guy, Corey Stevens, Honey Boy Edwards, and Taj Mahal. Headliners in 1999 included Kenny Wayne Shepherd, John Hammond, Robin Ford, and the amazing Robert Lockwood Jr., 89-year-old son of the father of the acoustic blues in the Mississippi Delta. Fender, the main sponsor, is a foremost manufacturer of acoustic guitars.

A September Surf Music Festival was inaugurated in 1998 with Dick Dale, King of the Surf guitar, the Chantays, and the Blue Hawaiians. In 1999, Dick Dale was joined by The Stingrays, a teenage group continuing the surf tradition.

Broadcasting from the Casino

During construction, an elaborate sound system was built into the Casino so that music from the dance orchestras or the theater organ could be piped throughout the building or broadcast over Avalon Bay. The sound carried overpoweringly well over the bay, so public broadcasting was attempted only occasionally. However, the sound of music from the fabulous new ballroom was soon heard from coast to coast over radio.

Philip K. Wrigley was a friend of Les Atlas, president of Columbia Broadcasting System, which had its main studios and offices in the Wrigley Building in Chicago. In 1934, Mr. Wrigley arranged for nightly broadcasts of dance music from the Casino Ballroom. At the time, CBS and the other national networks, NBC and MBS, aired live dance music regularly, and a growing number of orchestras were gaining nationwide reputations from radio shows.

Thus, at 9:30 on the evening of May 15, 1934, listeners across the nation heard the voice of Don McBain announce, "From the beautiful Casino Ballroom, overlooking Avalon Bay at Catalina Island, we bring you the music of…" The names of the bands changed regularly, the announcers became more involved in the fun of the programs, and the broadcasts continued with few interruptions to the 1950's.

Generally speaking, in the 1930s, music from the ballroom was aired in two half-hour segments, from 9:30 to 10 and from 11 to 11:30 p.m. Locally, the music was heard over KHJ, a station within the Don Lee Broadcasting System, which was a part of the CBS Pacific Coast System. Segments were also broadcast over the nationwide CBS network. It was this exposure that helped Jan Garber on his way to fame in the summer of 1934.

Ben Bernie, who had his own show for Lucky Strike in 1935, broadcast over NBC from the Hotel St. Catherine at dinnertime before moving on to the Casino where his music went out over CBS. The bandleaders had become stars. They chatted with other film and radio celebrities over the airways and attracted well-known guest performers. Little Jack Little, with a show for Chesterfield, had a large radio following on CBS by the time he played the Casino in 1936.

Air time was not limited to dance music. The cross-channel Aquaplane Races were broadcast from the Casino over MBS in 1937, announced by Gary Breckner, who had a long and happy association with Avalon. An air show, "Life of the Party," was heard Sunday nights from the Casino on KNX in the CBS Pacific Coast System. Herbie Kay's dinner broadcast from Hotel St. Catherine also went out nightly over that station during his engagement.

Gary Breckner was master of ceremonies for a four hour special "Catalina Summer Show of 1938," which opened the Casino for the season. This featured a well-known radio conductor, Lud Gluskin, and his 16 piece CBS orchestra, transported especially for the occasion, plus numerous Hollywood stars. The arrival of each new orchestra had become a gala affair with welcoming parades and star-studded opening nights. The band

DANCE YOUR CARES AWAY
WITH THE *Melody Master*

Listen in every night
at 9:30 and 11:00 over
KHJ
and the Don Lee Network

Hal
GRAYSON
AND HIS ORCHESTRA

NOW AT THE
SANTA CATALINA ISLAND *Casino*
EVERY NIGHT AND SUNDAY AFTERNOONS

WT Co. 33

leaders also developed specialty spots with games, patter, and song quizzes, and encouraged audience participation. Dick Jurgens featured a "Musical Cookbook" on Wednesday nights during his 1938 tour.

The "College of Musical Knowledge," Kay Kyser's show for the American Tobacco Company, was broadcast from the Avalon Theatre from 6 to 7 p.m. every Wednesday over NBC, and his dance music was aired nightly from the ballroom over CBS, during his engagements at the Casino

Ted Weems' *Heading for Catalina show*, 1939
(announcer Gary Breckner on left)

in 1939 and 1940. Tickets to his Wednesday show were free, and the waiting line stretched the length of Casino Way.

Ted Weems started a new Sunday night radio show in 1939, "Heading for Catalina," which aired on KNX. The Sunday night fun show during the Goodman and Jurgens tours in 1940 was "Catalina Dipsy Derby," a musical quiz in racing format, with Gary Breckner as master of ceremonies. Every night the

Benny Goodman at the *Catalina Dipsy Derby*, 1940

"Catalina Musical Mailbag" was opened and messages from Catalina visitors were sent to their friends over KNX.

Bob Crosby broadcast his "Camel Caravan" from Avalon Theatre every Thursday afternoon and evening during his engagements in 1940 and 1941. In 1940, the theater also hosted a session of the "P.D.Q. Quiz Court," normally broadcast from the stage of the Paramount Theater in Los Angeles. Contestants were picked at random and queried by Catalina's favorite announcer, Gary Breckner. Dick Jurgens broadcast his "Fitch Bandwagon" program from the theater on Sunday afternoons during his 1941 tour.

During World War II, broadcasting from the Casino continued. The dedication ceremonies for the U.S. Maritime Services Training Center at Avalon were broadcast over MBS on December 15, 1942. Lt. Phil Harris, leader of the USMS band, provided music. Many of the USO entertainments for the servicemen went out over CBS by way of KNX and also over the Armed Forces Network as shortwave transmissions worldwide. Abe Lyman broadcast from "Island X" for the "Victory Parade" program sponsored by Coca Cola in 1942.

In addition, a series of regular programs emanated from the Casino. The USMS program, "We Deliver the Goods," featuring a patriotic script and music of the Maritime Band, led by Lt. Harris, then by Lt. Curt Roberts,

Lt. Curt Roberts and the USMS Band, WW II

was produced in Avalon Theatre, with Sam Brandt as announcer. It was aired continuously for 96 weeks coast to coast over CBS before signing off for the last time from the Casino on September 15, 1945.

The Big Band sounds from the Casino Ballroom were again heard regularly over CBS during the summer of 1946 and also continued to go out over the Armed Forces Network. In addition, announcer Cliff Johnson interviewed celebrities and visitors arriving on the steamers. The Bob Hope

USMS Chorus singing for the wartime nationwide radio show *We deliver the Goods*

ON THE AIR

How 19-year-old Radio Operator Kenneth Morgan of Princetown, Kentucky, who was only two weeks out of the U. S. Maritime Service Training Station at Gallups Island, Massachusetts when his ship was torpedoed, stuck to his post sending out an SOS—culminating in the rescue of ten of the members of the crew, will be retold over the CBS-U.S. Maritime Service program, "We Deliver The Goods," next Sunday.

The ship's master, Captain Walter E. Reed, pays particular tribute to the value of Maritime Service training in commenting on the fact that this was Morgan's first trip, as an officer since his graduation from the Gallups Island Maritime Service radio school.

Musical highlight of the program will be a Cole Porter medley presented by Lieut. Curt Roberts' U.S. Maritime Service Training Station Band, with Seaman First Class Robert Miessner supplying the vocals.

— WE DELIVER THE GOODS — although broadcast to the Columbia network (CBS) at 2130 may be heard by listeners in the KNX area at 2230. KNX is 1060 on your dial. Home Folks! Please consult your local newspaper for the time and station carrying the USMS program — WE DELIVER THE GOODS —

---

excerpt from USMS *Off Soundings*, 1945
CIM Collection

Show was aired from the Avalon Theatre in 1948 as a benefit for Rotary International. Gene Autry (and his horse) also did a show from the ballroom that year. Old favorite Jan Garber once more sent his music coast to coast over CBS during his long 1949 engagement. The next year, Roy Rogers and Dale Evans aired a show from the ballroom over the same station. Regular CBS radio broadcasts continued with announcer Ken Robinson and later Dave Young until 1951.

In 1952, KBIG, with transmitters located on Catalina, went on the air, and music from the ballroom could occasionally be heard at 740 on the local radio dial. KBIG's tall announcer, Carl Bailey ("Mr. Big"), became a very popular master of ceremonies at various Avalon functions. He sometimes broadcast the Miss Catalina Beauty Contest from Avalon Theatre.

Music could also still be

heard sporadically over CBS until 1963, and one summer over KEZY. Then the Big Band era was over. Radio broadcasts rarely emanate from the Casino nowadays and are usually local, such as a KLAC broadcast of a Country Western Jamboree in 1978.

Television broadcasts from Avalon enjoyed a brief popularity in 1950, when a 13-week series was seen on KFI-TV. Segments were shot on the glass bottom boat, from the Pleasure Pier, and at Casino Point. Glimpses of the Casino are still frequently seen on television for it is effectively used as background to lend glamour to fashion and automobile commercials. It has also been used as a setting for episodes in TV series such as *Mannix, Cannon,* and *Quincy.* During a 1985 episode of *Airwolf,* the building was attacked so convincingly by sinister movie helicopters that the studio was charged for a new coat of paint.

In 1983, the New Year's Eve Gala was broadcast nationwide as part of the Dick Clark coverage for KABC. At 9 p.m., balloons dropped from the ceiling and orchestra leader Alvino Rey obligingly played *Auld Lang Syne* to synchronize with the time difference on the East Coast. At midnight, balloons dropped again for the "real" New Year's Eve. Musician John Tesh staged a benefit concert in the Casino ballroom for Public Television in 1996 that included a spectacular light show on the building. This hour-long spectacle was seen around the nation during pledge drive.

Since 1996, a glimpse of the interior of Avalon Theatre can be seen in theaters abroad whenever an MGM film is shown. Joseph, the MGM lion, traveled to the island that year to trot obediently down the theater aisle and onto the stage to poke his head through a screen and roar, creating MGM's logo for European film distribution.

Closer to home, Avalon's favorite weatherman, Los Angeles KNBC-TV's Christopher Nance, who is a popular master of ceremonies and supporter of local benefits, often treats his viewers to glimpses of the Casino, usually bathed in Catalina sunshine.

11 Managing the Casino

The Santa Catalina Island Company built and still owns the Casino. William Wrigley Jr. considered Avalon and Santa Catalina Island as a resort entity with all of the parts functioning to support the whole. The Casino was meant to function as an attraction to the Island by providing entertainment and enjoyment. It was not envisioned as being an independently profitable venue. In the ensuing years, as tastes as well as the scope of the Santa Catalina Island Company changed, the maintenance and management of this magnificent building has presented unique challenges.

Company general manager D. M. Renton had overall responsibility for the operation of the Casino during its first years. Tom White, a Hollywood promoter who held the lease on Avalon's Riviera Theatre, leased the new Avalon Theatre in 1929 and also signed on as general manager of the Casino operation. His lifestyle proved too flamboyant, and his association with the Casino ended in December of 1929.

Art LaShelle, who had managed the Riviera and Avalon Theatres for Tom White, stayed on to manage both theaters and the facilities for the expanding movie and yachting colony at the Isthmus until 1939. He was popular on the Island and was always hobnobbing with the movie stars and yachtsmen.

L. M. (Tommy) Thomas, who had started as a projectionist in 1932, developed into assistant manager, then became manager of the theaters from 1939 to 1948, with a break during World War II when he managed the Riviera Theatre for the local civilian population. Western Amusement Company (headed by Ted Jones and later his wife, Peggy) leased the theater in 1949 and operated it as part of their mainland theater chain until 1987 when the Santa Catalina Island Company resumed direct management. Tommy Clements and his wife Sally managed the theater for Western Amusement Company for the 38 years it held the lease.

The Casino Ballroom was operated within the general structure of the Santa Catalina Island Company until 1934. Larry Paper was the ballroom floor manager from 1929 to 1933. Concessions such as the soda fountain, check rooms, and pottery shop were leased to various individuals to operate.

Catalina Concessions Company was formed as a subsidiary of Santa Catalina Island Company in 1934 to operate Catalina resort features such as the hotels, glass bottom boats, and Casino. The steamship line (Wilmington Transportation Co., later renamed Catalina Island Steamship Line, and then Catalina Island Sightseeing Lines) bore the cost of operating the ballroom. The Santa Catalina Island Company functioned as landlord. Vice-president Harry Slaugh was responsible for the Casino. Ballroom managers under his supervision included Lew C. Oesterle, 1935-37, and Virgil Myers, 1938-1939.

General maintenance of the building was the responsibility of William Bowman, an electrician by trade, who lived in an apartment in the south wing of the building from 1929 to 1946 and functioned as general building superintendent.

The U.S. Maritime Service leased the building during World War II to use for training classes and entertainment for recruits. After the war, Catalina Concessions Company resumed operation of the ballroom with Ray Nichols as manager in 1946. By 1947, Malcolm Renton, who had been with the Santa Catalina Island Company since 1929, returned from service as a captain in the U.S. Army, and, following in his father's footsteps, became vice-president and secretary of the Company, positions he held until his retirement in 1975. Dale Eisenhut, who became building superintendent in 1947, reported directly to him.

The ballroom was remodeled and operated as a restaurant, with dancing, during the summer of 1948, with Fred Weiszmann as manager. This was not a financially successful venture and Catalina Island Steamship Line declined to finance the ballroom operation in 1949. The Avalon Chamber of Commerce raised funds to provide bands for the season, and the Company made the ballroom available. Larry Paper was manager for the first half of the season; Dale Eisenhut, for the second half. In 1950, the Company and the steamship line carried the entire cost of operating the ballroom under manager Jack Smith.

Herman D. Hover (from Ciro's in Hollywood) leased the ballroom in 1951, with Robert K. Smiley as manager. This operation lasted only one season, and the ballroom remained "dark" in 1952, except for benefit dances and conventions.

From 1953 to 1957, the City of Avalon sponsored dances in the ballroom from July through Labor Day each year. The Chamber of Commerce organized pre-season Saturday night dances. Wilfred F. Olsen, who had been managing various Company hotel operations since 1935, headed the City-sponsored committee that selected the bands. Dale Eisenhut managed the operation of the ballroom. During 1958-59, Eisenhut leased and operated the ballroom himself.

Channel Concessions Company, a subsidiary of MGRS, Inc., a corporation that leased and later bought the SS *Catalina,* operated the ballroom as part of its lease from 1960 to 1965 and provided dancing during the summer. Leonhardi Catering Company leased the ballroom from 1964 to 1986, renting it out for dances and conventions and providing fine catering services for these functions.

Dale Eisenhut remained as building superintendent from 1947 until his death in 1980. Frank Buck replaced him in that position until 1986. In 1987, the Santa Catalina Island Company named Billy Delbert as Director of Casino Operations. In that same year, the Company resumed operation of both the theater and the ballroom, making Delbert responsible for both maintenance and operation of the building. Delbert brought to the position twenty years of experience in entertainment management.

In 1988, Paxson Offield, a great grandson of Casino builder William Wrigley Jr., became president of the Santa Catalina Island Company (advancing from a vice president). He was well aware that the grand old building was beginning to show her age and soon after the hiring of Billy Delbert began a serious planning effort to restore her to her full glory. This involved a major renovation of the structure and a plan to rejuvenate the building as a magnet to attract visitors to the Island.

Delbert began operating the theater when Western Amusement Company's lease expired in 1987. When Leonhardi's lease expired that same year, the Company entered into a catering lease with Tom Campanelli and Larry Buster of a well-known local eating establishment, Ristorante Villa Portofino, lasting for about a year and a half. Larry Buster continued the lease for a short time, then catering was provided until 1993 by Dudley Morand and Bill Johnson, who had operated the Catalina Visitors Country Club for the Santa Catalina Island Company until it was closed for earthquake retrofitting.

CIM Collection

An Avalon Lancers home game in the ballroom

The costly renovation of the building proceeded at a measured pace, with major projects scheduled for the winter season in order to interfere with entertainment activities as little as possible. However, the building was quite busy during the winter of 1988-89, serving a most unusual need. That year, during school basketball season, the ballroom was home court for the Avalon Lancers. A regulation basketball court (84 x 50 ft.) was taped off on the historic dance floor and portable baskets were set up. To provide adequate lighting, Billy Delbert had banks of theatrical lights temporarily installed. The lighting frames also served to protect the historic chandelier.

This is but one example of a long history of the Company's responsiveness to community needs. This time the school gymnasium was being demolished because of its asbestos content and the team, which is extremely important to the small community, would have had nowhere to play until construction of the new gym was complete. Painting of the ballroom was delayed until the following year.

The building renovation included extensive upgrading of plumbing and electrical systems (including changing from quaint old-fashioned fuses to modern circuit breakers) as well as the more visible painting and restoration described throughout this book. The Company's purpose is to make the Casino a useful and attractive venue for public and private special events that will attract visitors to the Island and thus continue to provide the pleasure for which it was originally designed.

In 1989, the Santa Catalina Island Company had developed, in consultation with the community and the City of Avalon, a 15-year plan designed to utilize its properties for the mutual best interests of all concerned. One element of the plan, which received approval from the California Coastal Commission in 1993, called for creating a first-class resort complex in Descanso Canyon (north of the Casino) former site of the famed Hotel St. Catherine. The Casino building was seen as an integral part of the new resort.

The Pointe Corporation was awarded the option to develop the resort complex and as part of the project leased the ballroom from 1993 to 1995. The Pointe also assumed operation of Descanso Beach Club and the Catalina Visitors Country Club as part of their venture. When an economic recession made capital scarce and the proposed development didn't materialize, P. Offield Enterprises (POE) assumed the leases in September of 1995. Santa Catalina Island Company president Paxson Offield formed POE as an independent company to assure uninterrupted operation of the facilities until prospects for resort development improved.

Billy Delbert continued as Director of Casino Operations for the Santa Catalina Island Company and also became the first president of POE until it was fully organized. (He has also had direct management of Avalon Theatre since 1987.) POE has since morphed into Catalina Island Resort Services. CIRS leases the ballroom to event producers such as Art Good, who puts on the very successful annual Jazz Trax Festival. It also puts on events itself working through Chee Productions, headed by Chee Ammen (whose association with the Casino goes back to 1986 when he worked for Art Good in developing Jazz Trax). Chee Productions is responsible for the annual Blues and Surf Festivals and also books other entertainment into the ballroom and other CIRS venues.

In 1929, William Wrigley Jr. envisioned the Casino as an attraction within the framework of the entire resort community of Avalon and the Island, not as a self-supporting venue. So it has remained. As large as they may seem, neither the ballroom nor the theater can accommodate the stadium-size crowds that make modern musical events profitable. The Casino operation itself will never recoup the cost of its over $1,535,000 renovation and continual upkeep. The Company regularly makes the ballroom or theater available for community events such as nonprofit benefits or high school graduation at little or no cost and often negotiates liberal terms (of less than optimal profitability) in order to secure commercial events that will bring business to the town.

The Santa Catalina Island Company takes its role of stewardship very seriously and, as a result, millions more visitors will be able to enjoy Avalon's magnificent and historic landmark in the 21st century.

Casino Residents

Few people were aware that there was an apartment at the top of the south wing of the Casino when it was occupied by building superintendent William Bowman from 1929 to 1946. However, when Dale Eisenhut and his wife, Donna, moved into the compact aerie, the situation soon changed with the advent of their three daughters.

Building superintendent Dale Eisenhut, his wife Donna and daughters Alice, Jani, and Lynn

In a few years, passers-by occasionally skipped a few heart beats if they happened to glance up and glimpse a child go tripping along the parapet or saw the two older girls dangle their little sister by her feet out of what amounted to a ten-story window. Then all three girls graduated to motorcycles, on which they roared up the Casino ramps to park at their "front door" on one side of the ballroom.

In spite of such irreverent behavior, Alice, Lynn, and Jani Sue graduated as valedictorians of their classes at Avalon Schools and went on to obtain university degrees. During their

Jani Eisenhut on the roof of her home

sojourn in the building, they added a delightfully human dimension and provided the guides on the Casino Tours with entertaining subject matter. Today, they consider it a privilege to have grown up in such a magnificent building.

Dale, who was an expert electrician and generally handy man, maintained the complex electrical system and with his helpers made all but the major repairs to the building. Known in certain circles as the "phantom of the Casino", he knew all the nooks, crannies, and tunnels of this incredible building. On the matter of policing and security, Dale noted that although he had to be alert to keep souvenir hunters from walking away with pieces of the building, there were very few attempts to deface the walls with graffiti. Apparently, most people had a natural respect for the beauty of the structure. (Perhaps the fact that Dale was a Los Angeles County Reserve Sheriff's Deputy helped a little.)

The Eisenhuts were active volunteers and soon became an integral part of the Avalon community. Donna was a substitute teacher at Avalon Schools and librarian for the Avalon Branch of the Los Angeles County Public Library for 27 years. After Dale's passing in 1980, she moved to a cottage in town with her daughter Jani Sue, who brings a unique historical perspective to her narration as a bus driver for Catalina Discovery Tours, a Santa Catalina Island Company operation.

Frank and Betty Buck occupied the Casino apartment during Frank's stint as building superintendent from 1980 to 1987, and instituted the position of Casino patrol dog—filled by their miniature schnauzer which marched dutifully around the building on his daily walks.

Billy Delbert Collection

Billy Delbert was a bachelor when he assumed the reins as Director of Casino Operations in 1987. His daughter, Tracia, lived with him for a time. While working as a waitress during a Jazz Trax Festival, she met sound man Brian Langowski and the couple were married in the Casino Ballroom. Actually, they were married on one side of the ballroom and drove a suitably bedecked golf cart around the outside balcony to their reception on the other side of the ballroom. Langowski now handles audio-visual matters in the Casino for the Santa Catalina Island Company.

Director of Casino Operations Billy Delbert, his wife Anni, and children Alexis and Rex

Over time, the romantic ambience of the Casino overcame Billy and he proposed to Anni Marshall, Director of Community Services for the City of Avalon. Anni is a "live-wire", always initiating and overseeing recreational activities and other community services for the community. Billy is in demand as a master of ceremonies. An avid fisherman, he also assists with the logistics of several local fishing derbies that raise funds for community youth organizations.

Their two children, Alexis and Rex, learned how to ride their bicycles in the privacy of the ballroom. Rex, being of a fearless nature (and constantly in a bruised condition), has been known to use the Casino ramps for skateboard practice.

Thoroughly modern children, both complain that the Casino is too far out of town. Alexis, however, as a teenager realized that there was a plum year round job just steps from her home. Accordingly, in the tradition of young Casino residents, she donned an Avalon Theatre polo shirt and began dispensing popcorn to moviegoers.

The family has two options for reaching their apartment—by ramp, if feeling the need for aerobic exercise, or by elevator, if not. Neither is quick. The Otis freight elevator proceeds at a leisurely pace and requires a strong and steady thumb on the button the whole time to keep it moving. Next to the elevator in the loading only zone there is a golf-cart-size rectangle painted on the pavement and marked "Resident Parking". On school mornings, the resident golf cart (containing children) has often been seen executing a tight U-turn and heading briskly for school on the other end of town.

Billy Delbert has become the new "phantom of the Casino." He is usually somewhere around the building but has to be found. He may be checking up on his maintenance crew, or keeping an eagle eye on a renovation project, or showing prospective clients the venue, or huddled over the computer planning for the future. His office is deep within the building and not accessible to the public, so when he is expecting visitors he can usually be seen hovering near the entrance to the theater or near the elevator waiting to meet them. This way of doing business may seem odd to mainlanders used to arriving at impressive offices and being greeted by pert receptionists, but it has been a tradition of the Casino for over 70 years.

12 Changing Times

Catalina is a Magic Isle. Life goes on from day to day and year to year with a rhythm of its own. In a state where few persons claim birthrights, the Island boasts third, fourth, and even fifth generation natives. There are also many families, some owning summer homes, who have vacationed on the Island for generations. Yet the magical island is tied to the world by tourism. Its fortunes depend on the vagaries of this industry, and events in the mainland world affect the island significantly. Even on Catalina, times change.

SCI Co. Collection

Casino Way, 1929

The Island's history has been characterized by spurts of development. In the 1890's, the town of Avalon grew rapidly from a single hotel and a few tents to a well-known watering place abustle with long skirted ladies carrying parasols and gentlemen who apparently fished wearing bowler hats. The misfortunes of fire and war brought on a decline. William Wrigley Jr. was riding a crest of national prosperity when he created a new wave of development in the 1920's. By the time of his death in early 1932, he had made good his promise to develop Catalina into the Play Isle of the Pacific and a place that ordinary people could afford.

However, when Philip K. Wrigley assumed responsibility for Catalina, the country was deep in depression. Even the attraction of the new Casino failed to maintain the all important visitor count. In response, steamer fares were reduced, as were lodging rates and theater tickets. William Wrigley Jr. had freely invested personal funds in the Island. Now a conservative bank was co-trustee of the estate. The Island enterprise had to make economic sense, and although dedicated firmly to his father's ideals, Philip K. Wrigley began to reorganize the sprawling Santa Catalina Island Company when the depression was at its worst. He placed the resort features, such as hotels, glass bottom boats, and Casino, within the framework of a new Catalina Concessions Company. The steamship line was expected to bear the cost of the operation of the Casino as a sightseeing attraction.

CIM Collection

Philip K. Wrigley on one of his fine Arabians

Philip Wrigley continued to improve the town. He cultivated the Early California atmosphere, remodeling Crescent Avenue into La Avenida Crescenta lined with palm and olive trees, a serpentine wall, and Spanish fountains. Troubadours in Spanish dress strolled around the town, playing Latin tunes. On visits to the Island, Mr. Wrigley and his family would often join local parades, riding Arabian horses from their ranch in the interior.

The El Encanto shops and Mexican restaurant were developed as an additional tourist attraction, as was the Isthmus colony. His continued attempts to develop Catalina into a year round resort were of little avail, but Mr. Wrigley established the successful pattern of engaging a series of the nation's top bands for the summer and arranged for nationwide broadcasts of their music. When the Big Band craze swept the nation in the 1930's, Catalina, with its beautiful Casino, entered another "golden age."

Catalina glittered with movie stars during the 1930's. The Isthmus was a favorite location for filming. Such classics as *Rain* (1932), with Joan Crawford; *Treasure Island* (1934), with Wallace Beery; *Mutiny on the Bounty* (1935), with Clark Gable; and *The Hurricane* (1937), with Jon Hall, were shot there. The social and yachting columns of the local newspaper read like a Hollywood *Who's Who* of stars, producers, and directors seen dining at Hotel St. Catherine, partying aboard their yachts, or dancing at the Casino.

CIM Collection

Via Casino in the 1930's

The Casino

Then, on December 7, 1941, Pearl Harbor was attacked, and the twinkling lights of Catalina were blacked out for the duration. The Island was closed to tourism, and the Great White Steamers sailed off to war, painted battleship gray. The SS *Catalina* and SS *Cabrillo* served as troop ships in San Francisco Bay, the SS *Cabrillo* never to return to the Island. The SS *Avalon* became a training ship but still plied her way through the submarine nets at San Pedro and across the channel to Catalina, which had become a training center for several branches of the service.

The movie colony at the Isthmus gave way to the U.S. Coast Guard; the U.S. Army Signal Corps manned a top secret radar station at Camp Cactus on the far side of the Island; and the Office of Strategic Services (OSS) trained agents in strictest secrecy at Toyon Bay. At Avalon, the U.S. Maritime Service trained 3,000 men every six weeks, using the Casino Building for classes as well as for entertainment.

World War II, of course, brought major changes to the entire world—not only changes in habits of living but also advances in technology that had wide-ranging effects. Larger and larger airplanes carried vacationers not only faster, but also farther away to exotic new vacation spots. Television revolutionized the movie industry and changed entertainment patterns. All of these forces had their impact on Catalina, but the most immediate effect of the war was that it left the Island with worn-out facilities.

The Santa Catalina Island Company, with some federal reimbursement for wartime depreciation, spent considerable sums attempting to remodel Hotel St. Catherine and refurbish its other facilities. Philip K. Wrigley expected no great profit from the Company, but he wanted it to be self supporting. It was time to retrench. In the late 1940's, with tourism in decline after its first postwar rush, the Island began a long period of readjustment.

The Santa Catalina Island Company began leasing various facilities to private individuals. However, it retained its sightseeing operations, building new glassbottom boats and modernizing its tour busses. The City of Avalon, which had been incorporated in 1913, began to assume more municipal responsibility, taking control of street cleaning and garbage collection, sewage disposal, utilities (later entrusted to Southern California Edison), and operation of the harbor.

Catalina gave its sons during the next two wars but not its land. The Island's economy responded to the nation's periods of prosperity and recession, and inhabitants dealt with water shortages during repeated droughts, but Catalina's well being was most directly dependent on the state of its cross-channel transportation. The SS *Avalon* was retired in 1951. Increasing costs and strikes kept the SS *Catalina* in berth during the winter (and an occasional summer), and smaller boats plied the channel in her stead. The steamship line no longer felt able to support such attractions as the Catalina Bird Park and the Casino Ballroom. The City of Avalon provided the Big Bands from 1953 to 1957.

Accommodations for visitors also decreased during this period. In 1957, the outmoded Island Villas (bungalettes for 2,500 people) were torn down. The Hotel St. Catherine followed in 1966 (along with the Catalina Bird Park). Las Casitas Bungalows and Pavilion Lodge, built by the Santa Catalina Island Company, and a scattering of small hotels built by various other businessmen did not make up for the loss in rooms. With transportation and accommodations curtailed, Catalina was again in decline. In 1965, Big Bands were no longer regularly scheduled during the summer in the Casino. However, there were already signs that times were about to change again.

Through these lean years, the real estate business was booming in Southern California. Tremendous pressures were being put on Mr. Philip K. Wrigley either to sell the Island or to develop it. Yet, he still felt strongly, as had his father before him, that Catalina should remain unspoiled, retaining its natural beauty for future generations. However, he did have a master plan prepared for limited development. The plan addressed the development of Company properties within the City of Avalon and at Two Harbors while leaving the interior as open space. The City of Avalon engaged the same planner, William L. Pereira and Associates. With State of California aid, the City of Avalon built breakwaters on each side of Avalon Bay that provided added protection during winter storms. The steamer pier was removed in 1968, and additional moorings for yachts installed.

The establishment of a Marine Science Center in Big Fisherman's Cove at Two Harbors (the Isthmus) on land donated to the University of Southern California by Mr. Wrigley was one of the first signs that a different kind of interest in Catalina was emerging. The Island's natural resources began receiving more attention, and new species of plants and animals were identified. As the mainland megalopolis became smoggier, the Island's clear waters and fresh air appeared ever more alluring in contrast. The experience of open spaces grew more precious, and Catalina beckoned.

This new national awareness of the importance of maintaining natural areas gave Mr. Wrigley his opportunity to ensure that the Island was preserved. In 1974, the Santa Catalina Island Company negotiated an open-space easement with Los Angeles County that would free the Island from some of the pressure for development. In 1975, the Wrigley and Offield families donated (by stock transfer) approximately 88% of the Island to the Santa Catalina Island Conservancy to be preserved and enjoyed as an open space area forever.

Fortunately, Catalina's transportation problem was being solved so that it was able to cater to this new interest. Catalina Island Cruises obtained a franchise from the Public Utilities Commission to operate passenger service from Long Beach in 1970 and from San Pedro in 1976, and visitor counts began to increase with the reestablishment of reliable, year round boat service. Catalina Express, with smaller, faster boats, began operations in 1983. Other boat operators appeared on the scene, and by the 1990s, visitors could also embark for Catalina from Dana Point and Newport Beach and travel by catamaran or single-hulled vessel. Regular helicopter service was also available.

The local tourist economy continues to be sensitive to regional and national fluctuations but, in general, it has been expanding as the visitor season has gradually been extended. The improved harbor accommodates more yachtsmen year around, and Catalina's Airport-in-the-Sky has become the busiest private airport on the West Coast. Cruise ships based in Los Angeles began including Avalon year round among their ports of call in 1988. Long gone are the days when local businesses could close for several months in the winter.

The Catalina Island Visitors Bureau and Chamber of Commerce has modernized its operations and now effectively promotes Catalina as a destination. More and more people are escaping to the Island throughout the year from an increasingly metropolitan mainland. Some come to run grueling marathons in the scenic hills, others to scuba dive in the remarkably clear waters, and many just to relax and breathe the fresh air. The local population is growing and real estate values reflect the increased interest in Island living.

When Philip K. Wrigley died in 1977, his son, William Wrigley, assumed the family responsibility on Catalina and became Chairman of the Executive Committee of the Santa Catalina Island Company. He personally continued to foster scientific interest in the Island by endowing the Wrigley Institute for Environmental Studies at the University of Southern California and funding expansion of its island station, the Wrigley Marine Science Center at Two Harbors. He also strongly supported the Santa Catalina Island Conservancy and the Wrigley Memorial and Botanical Garden, overseeing their eventual merger. The Conservancy, with its mission of conservation, restoration, and education, is assuring that Catalina will become an even more interesting and enjoyable place to visit for generations to come.

William Wrigley also initiated an extensive assessment and planning process (with input from the City of Avalon and the general community) that resulted in a 15-year plan for development. He tackled the problem of lack of accommodations, both for visitors and for residents, with the result that several condominium complexes were built on leased Santa Catalina Island Company land. The Company also undertook extensive renovation of its properties (conforming in the process to more stringent earthquake standards) and continues to actively seek a developer for a major resort complex. In the meantime, other hoteliers have expanded their modest meeting facilities and Avalon is attracting more small seminar and convention groups. Before his untimely death in 1999, William Wrigley had the satisfaction of knowing that his grandfather's magnificent Casino Building had been beautifully restored. Fortunately, the tradition of family stewardship continues. The future of the historic Casino is now in the hands of William Wrigley Jr. and Paxon Offield (William Wrigley Jr's. great grandson).

The Casino

Part of Catalina's attraction is scenic beauty and part is historic ambience. When the International Astronautical Federation, which included Russian and American astronauts, spent an evening in the Casino Ballroom during its 1976 convention, Bud Herrmann (formerly with the Benny Goodman orchestra) entertained them with the sounds of the Big Bands. The historical significance of the Casino attracted this international group as it has many others.

The theaters and ballrooms of the 1920s and 1930s are fast disappearing. Fortunately, the Catalina Casino survives, preserving the cultural heritage of an era in its concept and in its architecture. With age, it has added a new dimension to the pleasure it gives. The many visitors who join tours of the building appreciate it for its history as well as its unique beauty.

However, the Casino has not become a building just to be admired with reverence. It is still a lively "pleasure palace", although nobody would dream of using that phrase now. There is at least one major public event in the ballroom practically every month of the year. Its popularity for private corporate parties, weddings, and benefits is such that it is often booked far in advance. The venerable Casino has kept up with changing times.

A beauty to behold, the gracious lady still beckons, promising pleasure and marvelous memories to all who enter her portals.

Casino Tours

Prior to World War II, the Casino was occasionally included as part of sightseeing tours in Avalon, but for the most part the public has had access to the building only when attending an event such as a dance or a movie. Providing enough guards to allow general public access would be prohibitively expensive, and without guards, the building could not be preserved.

Great interest in the building finally led the Santa Catalina Island Company to begin regular Casino tours in June of 1972. These popular, 40 minute guided tours include the theater, mezzanine (where an exhibit about the history of the building has been mounted), ballroom, and balcony. Ticket information can be obtained at the Visitor's Information and Services Center, Box 1159, Avalon. Telephone: (310) 510-2500.

Catalina Island Museum

In 1953 a group of local citizens banded together to preserve the remarkable history of the Island and founded the Catalina Island Museum Society. The Santa Catalina Island Company generously leased space in the historic Casino Building, residents donated a variety of historical artifacts, volunteers staffed the facility, and so was born the Catalina Island Museum.

At the beginning of the twenty-first century the museum has grown to become a facility that exhibits and cares for over 100,000 artifacts and employs a staff of 9. For a modest admission fee, visitors are treated to exhibits that illustrate many facets of the Island's 7,000 years of history. Catalina pottery and tile are a highlight as are the exhibits that show the lifeways of the first inhabitants of the Island known as the Gabrielino/ Tongva or Pimuvit. Don't miss the exhibit on Catalina's steamships (including models of the beloved Great White Steamer, the S.S. *Catalina;* audio station with oral history reminiscences; and video of the steamers and passengers in the 1920s, 30s, and 40s), or the ranching exhibit where children can feel buffalo fur and sheepskin. In September, an annual exhibit of Catalina tile and pottery fills the museum and throughout the month artist demonstrations, walking tours, and a lecture series highlight and celebrate the unique history of Catalina Clay Products. The Museum also has an extensive research library that includes thousands of photos, books and ephemera which is available to researchers by appointment.

As part of its efforts to preserve and interpret Catalina's fascinating heritage, the Museum conducts research and oral history interviews and offers free lectures as well as group tours and educational programs. A corps of dedicated gallery docents is available to answer visitors' questions. It publishes *The Casino* book, *Avalon Walk-About*, a guide to walking tours in Avalon and *The Art of Catalina Clay Products*, a catalog of the Museum's pottery collection.

The Museum also hosts an open house of the former Wrigley mansion, now known as the Inn on Mt. Ada, during early December. In late spring the Museum puts on its main fundraising event, the highly entertaining and educational Silent Film Benefit. The Museum Store offers many educational and enjoyable items including books, Big Band CD's and cassettes, posters, reproduction Catalina tile, videos and T-shirts.

The Museum is a private, nonprofit 501(c)(3) corporation, supported through a combination of earned income through admissions, memberships, and store sales and support through grants and donations. The Museum welcomes inquiries and may be contacted at: Catalina Island Museum, P.O. Box 366, Avalon, CA 90704. Phone: 310-510-2414, FAX: 310-510-2780, email: museum@catalinas.net.

Catalina Art Association

The Catalina Art Association has maintained a gallery in the Casino since 1965 for exhibiting the work of member artists. The Association, formed in 1961, is comprised of artists, craftsmen, photographers, and their supporters. It sponsors art classes and often features demonstrations by local or visiting artists at its monthly meetings, which are open to the public.

Each year the Association sponsors the Catalina Art Festival in late September, a three day event during which Crescent Avenue becomes a huge gallery where mainland and even foreign artists display their work. A special invitational exhibit and a judges dinner is part of the festivities. Numerous cash prizes and ribbons are awarded. The year 2001 marked the 43rd Festival of Art.

The Catalina Art Association is a private, nonprofit corporation. It welcomes membership and support (tax deductible). Inquiries should be addressed to: Catalina Art Association, Box 235, Avalon, CA 90704.

Footnotes

1. Walter Webber, "Interesting Structural and Architectural Features of Avalon Casino Described," *Southwest Builder and Contractor,* October 25, 1929, p.30.

2. Sumner A. Spaulding, "The Pleasant Isle of Catalina, Developing Avalon as a California Seashore Pleasure Resort," *California Arts & Architecture,* XXVI, 5 (November 1929), p.74.

3. May 31, 1929. Malcolm J. Renton Collection.

4. June 25, 1928. Santa Catalina Island Company, Casino Records.

5. Alma Overholt, "Casino Opening Charms Visiting Crowd," *The Catalina Islander,* XVI, 22 (June 5,1929), p.1.

6. *Ibid.,* pp.1-2.

7. Memorandum, May 28, 1929. Malcolm J. Renton Collection.

8. April 15, 1929. Malcolm J. Renton Collection.

9. Maury Paul, letter to Lank Menge, n.d. [March 1979]. Lank Menge Collection.

10. July 5, 1932. Curt Houck Collection.

Selected Bibliography

Doran, Adelaide LeMert. *The Ranch that was Robbins'.* Los Angeles, 1963.

Overholt, Alma. *The Catalina Story.* Revised edition. Avalon, California, 1978.

Simon, George T. *The Big Bands.* Revised edition. New York, 1974.

Windle, Ernest. *Windle's History of Catalina.* Avalon, California, 1931.

The Catalina Islander (Avalon), Vols. 15-65 (1928-1999)

"Salient facts about the new Catalina Casino briefed for convenient reference," From the Publicity Bureau of the William Wrigley, Jr. Interests. Grand Opening, May 29, 1929. (10 page publicity pamphlet describing building). Catalina Island Museum, Casino Collection.

Water Lines, Quarterly Newsletter of the Santa Catalina Island Company, 1986-1999.

Avalon Bay News (Avalon), vols. 1-10 (1990-1999)

INDEX

Kay, Herbie, 89, 109
Kay, John, 105
Kaye, Danny, 92
Kaye, Mary, 96
KBIG, 33,66,74, 113
Keit, Richard, 48
Kenton, Stan, 94
KEZY, 114
KFI-TV 114
KHJ, 109
Kicks, The, 102
King Zulu Paraders, 100
Kiss, Alexander, 51
KLAC, 114
KNBC-Ty 114
Knudson, Professor Vern O., 44
KNX, 109, 111
Kosa, Emil Jr., 51
Kovert Hollywood Revue, 34
Krupa, Gene, 101
Kyser, Kay, 90, 92, 110
La Avenida Crescenta, 125
Lamour, Dorothy, 89
Lane, Frankie, 96
Lang, Johnny, 107
Langowski, Brian, 122
Las Casitas Bungalows, 128
LaShelle, Art, 35,115
LATOS (see American Theatre Organ
Society, L.A. Chapter), 57
Laurel, Stan, 59
Leonhardi Catering Company, 117-118
Lescht & Associates, Inc., 75
LeVitt, Barbara, 32
Liddell, Charles M., 36
Lions A Poppin!, 65
Little, Little Jack, 89, 109
Little Sugarloaf, 12, 14
Llewellyn Iron Works, 24
Llewellyn, David, 25
Lockhart, June, 97
Lockwood, Robert Jr., 107
Long Beach School District, 81
Long Beach Symphony Orchestra, 97
Longo, Pat, 101
Los Angeles County, 129
Los Angeles County Public Library, 121
Los Angeles County Sheriffs Department, 66,121
Los Angeles Da Camera Society, 64
Los Angeles Philharmonic Orchestra, 96
Lyman, Abe, 111
Mack, Jack, 103
MacKenzie, Giselle, 96
Malneck, Matty, 94
Man in the Iron Mask, 37
Manning, Norman, 34
Mannix, 114

Mar Dels, The, 100
March of Dimes Ball, 94
Marine Bar, 71, 79
Maritime Band, See USMS Band
Marshall, Anni, 122
Martin, Freddy, 90, 97-100
Martin, Tony, 96
Marta, Vernon, 72
Mary Kaye Trio, 96
Mason, Dave, 103
Matsui, Keiko, 105-106
Mattson, Alfa, 32
Matysek, Eva *(see also Eva Matysek Fine Art
Restoration)*, 53
Mayall, John, 105
Mayer, Louis B., 63
MBS, 108-109
McBain, Don, 109
McMillian, Mr., 32
McNeely, Big Jay, 104
Memo Bernabei Orchestra, 102
Menge, Lank, 35, 85-86
Menge, Maurice, 33, 35, 85
Mercer, Johnny, 92
Merlin Jazz, 103
Mertz, Sherwood, 55
Messiah, 65
Metro-Goldwyn-Mayer (MGM), 114
Metropole Hotel, *See Hotel Metropole*
Mexican Band, 35
Mick Fleetwood and His Zoo, 103
Miller Mood, 101
Miller, Danny, 64
Miller, Glenn, 98
Miller, Max, 72
Milt Herth Trio, 94
Miss Catalina, 31, 65
Miss Catalina (swimsuit company), 93
Miss Catalina Beauty Contest, 113
Mitchum, Robert, 64
model railroad, 74
Modernaires, The, 101
Mohr, Bob, 94-95
mole, 16
Molina, Carlos, 92
Monroe, Vaughn, 101
Moon and Sixpence Ball, 95
Moore, Dwight, 72
Moorish, 21
Morand, Dudley, 118
Morgan, Jack, 98
Morgan, Russ, 96
Morituri, 64
Motorcycle Racers Ball, 94
Motorcycle races, 95
murals, 41, 45-54
Music in the Miller Mood, 101

The Casino